great supp... y
Kenyan kids.
Love from
Michael & Linda

Under the
Acacia Tree

CES Family of Friends

M. Frednikson
02/2021

◆ FriesenPress

Suite 300 - 990 Fort St
Victoria, BC, V8V 3K2
Canada

www.friesenpress.com

Copyright © 2020
'Stories of Acceptance, Gratitude, Compassion and Generosity'
Written by: CES Canada Family of Friends
Director: Michael Frederiksen
Editor: Carl Friesen
Photographer: Patricia Nyanchama Makori
Book Cover Art: 'Unwavering Solitude' by Michael Frederiksen
First Edition — 2020

ISBN

978-1-5255-5940-2 (Hardcover)
978-1-5255-5941-9 (Paperback)
978-1-5255-5942-6 (eBook)

Education, Philosophy & Social Aspects

Distributed to the trade by The Ingram Book Company

REVIEWS

"The reality of students unable to pay school fees is a major challenge in rural western Kenya. There are few charities that have supported our young people in their secondary education to the extent CES has. This book reveals how partnership and design mixed with love and compassion can free Kenyan families from acute poverty."

Sarah Awinja Ayumba
Sub-County Director of Education, Navakholo

"*Under the Acacia Tree* is an inspiring account of how a small Canadian charity has changed the lives of thousands of Kenyan students and their families. The story of CES shows that, even in an era of cynicism and disillusion, those trapped by poverty and injustice have reason to hope for a better life. This highly readable book will introduce you to the day-to-day challenges faced by the Third World, and also to realistic, on-the-ground solutions that groups like CES have made possible."

Bernard Simon, former correspondent, Financial Times
Fellow, Munk School of Global Affairs, University of Toronto

"Canada has played a huge role in the development of education and community health in Kenya. Part of that legacy is the work of CES Canada in western Kenya. The impact of a new generation of capable, confident and compassionate graduates will lead to a stronger, better Kenya."

HE Simon Nabukwesi,
Former Ambassador, Kenya High Commission to Canada

"This book shows that even the smallest donation to a charity can make a huge difference to an entire community. CES has invested in the education and wellbeing of youth living in poverty in western Kenya. So if you are tired of the daily routine and you want to make a difference, let this book inspire you."

Ron 'Ali D'Haeri' Ward,
Development Officer, CBM (Kenya)

"CES in Kenya has provided bright, needy students with an opportunity to learn and achieve a secondary education. This book tells the story of Kenyan youth locked in by barriers of poverty and gender bias and are now free through the power of education."

Mary Stella Maloba Chitechi
Former Principal Bishop Sulumeti Girls HS, Kakamega

UNDER THE ACACIA TREE IS DEDICATED TO

In memory of Sharyn Poole, humanitarian and CES Canada volunteer.
She died in Kakamega, Kenya on June 26, 2013 in her 69th year.
Loved by the those who called her 'Mommy', Sharyn's legacy
is one of hope, faith and love.

and

the 'Orphan Kids of Kakamega,'
the real heroes in the fight against HIV/AIDS.
They have faith and courage beyond comprehension.
The devastating effects of HIV/AIDS surround them;

yet they face each crisis with the hope that tomorrow will be better.

IMAGINE

Imagine a place where children of different colour, race,
creed or place of birth
are embraced, cherished, loved
where learning is a right and life is more than living
on the edge of survival
Imagine

Imagine a place where children with differences in
language or dialect speak freely without fear of prejudice
and ridicule from a mother tongue not their own
Imagine

Imagine a place where children rise above the pangs
of hunger, ravages of war and violent loss of innocence
knowing that for them something has been prepared
Imagine

Imagine a place where children have access to clean water
and diets far better than sugar cane or scraps of
rotting food
removed from the daily routines
searching, begging
Imagine

Imagine a place where children can dream
one day to find their identity in a society
that values their unique contribution and ability
Imagine

Imagine a place where children are children
not forced to parent younger siblings,
or displaced without inheritance
Imagine

Imagine a place where children are invited to learn
encouraged to discover their talent, set free to engage
in their own story of hope
Imagine

Imagine a place called CES

Under the Acacia Tree Anthology
09/2010

Table of Contents

Part V Towards Social Justice 177

FACES

Faces
Beautiful faces, pure faces,
Smiling faces, sad faces
Sacred faces, alive with hope.

I see your face,
I want to know your story
Cry when you cry, laugh when you laugh.

The beauty of Mt. Kenya,
Majesty of the Great Rift Valley,
Masai Mara stretching to infinity
Kakamega Rainforest, Nandi Escarpment
Jade sea of Turkana

Cannot compare to the face of one
who laughs in the face of poverty.

Face reflects your heart,
Eyes mirror your soul,
When I see your face
I see the heart of God.

Dedicated to the Orphan Kids of Kakamega
Under the Acacia Tree Music
04/2011

INTRODUCTION

"The true meaning of life is to plant trees, under whose shade you do not expect to sit."

- Nelson Henderson, Canadian author

And that's exactly what Community Education Services (CES) Canada has been doing since 2003, creating shade. The shade that protects and renews hope, the kind of shade that heals and restores lives. Hundreds of Kenyan youth have sat under the umbrella of CES, their lives transformed. To attend secondary school and achieve the KCSE Diploma was once an impossible dream. Now each has his or her own unique story to tell, all sharing a common thread, "Without CES we would never be where we are today."

The most prolific tree in Kenya, so distinctive with its flat top and dome shaped features, is the iconic acacia tree. Sunset photos with the acacia silhouette have become part of the beauty and mystique of the Kenyan landscape.

Acacias have a magnificent history of natural survival, with qualities that continue to create a stable environment for man, other living creatures and plant life. Some acacia species will grow up to twenty metres tall and live up to two hundred years, with one tap root digging deep, sometimes to a depth of sixty metres or more.

So, how does the title of this book relate to the work of CES?

When I first travelled to Kenya, I lived three months in the North East desert area near the border of Somalia. I struggled with what I witnessed. Acute poverty, gender inequalities, youth unemployment, early childhood mortality, women and children suffering from disease and malnutrition, lack of access to health, education, clean water and basic food supplies.

While consulting and doing research on the impact of HIV/AIDS on Kenya's school system, I also had the privilege of teaching at Garissa Boys HS. Most evenings we relaxed outdoors underneath the largest acacia tree in the school compound. A large woven rug made of goat and camel hair was spread over the sand to keep us dry from the moisture rising from the desert floor. Oppressively hot even at midnight, there was little to be gained by sleeping.

The moon cast long shadows behind us. Through the acacia's leaves and arm-like branches, the Milky Way poured its soft light on this gathering of mostly teachers and their families.

I was struck by the fact that all life here hung in the balance. Vulnerable and living on the edge of life, a survival of the fittest described the life cycle of every living being. I remember being overwhelmed by the power of nature and the reality of man's frailty. For me the acacia tree had become a filter to the universe above, surrounding us with its own brand of peace and security.

And that's the reason for the title of this book. The acacia tree represents a place where one can rest, learn, be refreshed and then move on. Just as the acacia blossoms when the rains come at long last, so too our students can blossom through new and unexpected learning opportunities. Under the acacia tree there is life, laughter and play, an apt way to describe our work in Kenya.

CES Canada in partnership with CES Kenya is like the acacia tree, providing the right environment and nutrients to nurture and water the fertile soil of learning for eager minds. Its mission is to alleviate poverty and provide access to education for needy and bright youth orphaned or affected by the HIV/AIDS pandemic. Over the past fifteen years, CES has reached out to marginalized and disadvantaged youth, casting a wide shadow to allow three thousand young people to sit under its shade.

That's the beauty and the magic of the acacia, also the promise and purpose for CES in Kenya. Young people nurtured by the CES family will mature and blossom; and like the acacia, with persistence and patience, they will grow to shelter and nurture others.

I hope *'Under the Acacia Tree'* will challenge your world view. Be inspired and join the growing number of people who are passionate about making their world a better place. You can be the shade that others so desperately need.

Under the Acacia Tree

Come, all who are weary
suffering from a life of pathos
living on the edge of survival
under the brutal sun
where hope is sucked dry
by the tyranny of time

Come, nomads seeking water
fighting a life of fear
in Ifo, Hagaderra, Dagahaly
refugee families at Dadaab Camp
struggling to survive
on forty Kenyan shillings a day
scarred by cruel fate

Come, poor and neglected ones
burdened by a life of loneliness
women and children held captive
by chains of endless abuse
hunger, TB, HIV/AIDS, death
daily reminders of a hopeless existence

Come, you who are desperate
with no plan for tomorrow
relocation a dying dream
tears all shed
wells of promise now dry

Come, find rest, shelter
under the acacia tree
where life is precious
shade creates laughter and play
healing thrives in desert's harshness
canopy deflects the burning ray

Under the Acacia Tree Anthology
07/2004

FOREWORD:

Why This Book Matters

by Carl Friesen, Editor

This book will help you understand how you can make a difference in the world. It's told through the voices of people who have made a huge difference to the lives of others. You will also hear first hand from those who have been helped, and who in many cases, have gone on to help others.

Through these pages, you'll get a better idea of how you can find a need and fill it, your way. You'll learn through our story about the first fifteen years of CES, a Kenya-Canada partnership.

So, this book has three main purposes: first, it's a record of what CES has been doing in Kenya since 2003. Second, it's an acknowledgement of the efforts of the many people who have made it all happen. Third, we hope that by describing our mission and its impact on literally thousands of people, others may want to get involved and support our work in Kenya.

HOW CES FITS INTO THE PICTURE:

I'm writing this on Canada Day, our national holiday, a day when I feel grateful for all of the unearned privileges and advantages I've received through the genetic lottery of being born in Canada. I had a chance to grow up in a peaceful, wealthy country that provides good quality free primary and secondary education to all. Almost all of our schools have reliable supplies of safe water, and dependable electricity. Students, for the most part, have the food at home that they need to provide the energy to study.

Yet I'm also well aware that due to the genetic lottery, many people in other countries don't have these advantages, through no fault of their own. So while "social justice" is a loaded term for many people, that's how I see CES – it's a chance to redress the balance, just a little bit, by giving opportunities to other people who don't have access to them.

CES started as the brainchild of two people – one from Kenya, the other from Canada who saw an unfair lack of opportunity in western Kenya, and decided to do something about it. That "something" was to provide scholarships to Kenyan youth who have been impacted by HIV/AIDS. How that came about – well, I'll let Malik, Michael and others tell that story in the pages to come.

SETTING THE STAGE: EDUCATION IN KENYA

It could be that like me, you grew up in a part of the world where education is provided by trained and well-paid teachers, in schools that are safe and well equipped, where everyone can attend without paying additional fees. Kenya has ambitions to provide that as well, but it's not all the way there yet.

CES started at a time when Africa had many children who had lost one or both parents due to HIV/AIDS. Some were being raised by grandparents or other relatives, and there were many child-led families, where the elder children cared for the younger as best they could. There was a pressing need for them to get an education.

Elementary and secondary education is generally available to all students in Kenya, although the quality of that free education varies greatly. Some of the schools are public, some private with many of them run through their religious affiliation.

CES has provided much-needed support for what Malik Khaemba described to me as "bright, needy and disciplined" students at the secondary as well as college and university levels. In 2008 the Kenyan government began providing increasing levels of support to high schools. Education is now, in the wonderful phrase I heard from one of the principals, "mostly free." This means that some school expenses are met, but students still must pay for such items as uniforms, books, lunches and transportation. High school is still well beyond the means of many Kenyan families, particularly rural families in the Kakamega area.

WHAT'S A MZUNGU?

In this book, I've occasionally used the term '*Mzungu says*' to start some explanatory text. It's an East African term for a White person of European descent. Friends from Africa living in Canada tell me it also gets thrown at them, as someone originally from Africa who moved to a First World country and now acts "white".

Some people think it's an insult. I don't. I love the explanation. The term comes from an insect that buzzes around one's head – 'zoom zoom zoom', looking terrifically busy, but not really getting anything done. I've also heard that the term comes from a Kiswahili word meaning spinning around in one place, which is kind of the same thing.

HOW TO READ THIS BOOK:

'*Under the Acacia Tree*' is set in rough chronological order, starting with the story of what started CES, and on to the present day. But it's not a narrative in the conventional sense. For you to understand CES, I need to get out of the way and let you hear the voices of the people involved. That includes a whole host of people who have had a role in making CES what it is today.

This means you can start reading the book pretty much anywhere – it's written in short, stand-alone chunks. You will enjoy a mix of poetry, story telling prose and reality descriptions of life in Kenya. Some of the voices you will hear have a uniquely Kenyan turn of phrase. In most cases, the text of the book comes from people who have done their own writing; in others, the stories are based on interviews that have been transcribed, with some light editing. There's a glossary at the back for terms that non-Kenyan readers might not know.

So please sit, read and enjoy the shade – '*Under the Acacia Tree*'.

Part I

Beyond the Comfort Zone

CHAPTER 1:
Take a Seat

Bora maisha; mengine ni majaliwa
"Life is the best gift; the rest is extra"

(Swahili expression)

Kenyans have a remarkable ability to laugh and remain positive, even when bad things are happening all around them. They understand the realities of poverty and powerlessness and inherently know that their only chance of survival is to embrace the long term. They live in hope of a better life. Waiting for something good to happen is as important as actually seeing the finished product. It's like the concept of faith, seeing something as completed when it really is not.

While visiting Namirama Girls HS in July 2012, Principal Granda Oprong' proudly showed me the new Computer Lab, pride of Navakholo sub-County. All I saw was the outside walls, a rectangle of red bricks rising fifteen centimetres above the ground. There was no infrastructure, windows or even a roof. The floor of the lab was grass and standing in the middle of the room was a tethered goat having a feed.

To Mdme Oprong', the project had already begun and it was only a matter of time until funding would permit the next stage of building the lab. Living in hope that one day things will all come together is a concept that *mzungu* has difficulty with. If you want to build, then get started. Don't wait until the funds are all there, for that will never happen.

Fast forward to October 2018 where I again visited Namirama Girls HS. I always enjoy this school, because it is the only one of our twenty-five schools where each time I visit, the Canadian flag greets me at the Admin block. This time I see the computer lab is built. Such a beautiful structure with office space, electricity, and a shiny treated cement floor. All it needs is some furniture, computers and an Internet hookup. All in good time, it will come, "O ye of little faith."

That's the problem with *mzungu*; actually, it is my problem. I am used to starting a project when the funding is in place. In Africa it seems to be the opposite. Kenya has taught me much about looking at life from a different perspective.

However, I still have trouble with these three words. Only in Kenya have I been so welcomed and ignored at the same time. "Take a Seat" is as common in East Africa as "may I help you," except the help part is missing. So what's wrong with a chance to rest, sit back and chill out. It should be a welcome pause in a busy day, until the realization that one is merely sitting with no end in sight. Despite an agreed upon appointment there is no meeting.

A cultural misunderstanding at best, one must realize that the meaning may differ between the one sitting and the one offering the seat. Taking a short rest should therefore not be misconstrued as a form of disrespect.

The Irish avant-garde playwright Samuel Becket wrote about two men waiting for a man named Godot. While Vladimir and his friend are hanging out, a boy shows up and tells him he is a messenger from Godot. He says that Godot will not be coming that evening but that he surely will come the next day. The next day the same, the boy enters and once again tells Vladimir that Godot will not be coming. He insists that he did not speak to Vladimir the day before. In this theatre of the absurd they wait in vain, nothing ever changes.

There's the rub - I wait and no one shows up. Like the characters in "Waiting for Godot", I try to make sense of it all by reflecting on my own personal experiences. That includes Kenya, where I wait, wait, and then wait some more. For Kenyans, waiting is as natural as breathing; waiting may even be a good thing because things might just improve as a result.

I recall the appointment made in early 2004 to meet with the Kenya Minister of Education in Nairobi. After three months living in Kenya, teaching and conducting research on the Impact of HIV AIDS on the Kenyan school system, I was now quite excited to share my findings. Arriving on time, I was told to take a seat. The Minister would be with me shortly. The same message three times over the next two hours tested my patience. Finally, a junior assistant ushered me into an office, accepted my written report, thanked me and promised that he would pass it on. I doubt that ever happened. I learned later that the Minister had never arrived, as he was in a meeting in Mombasa.

After 15 years of enjoying visits to Kenya, I have now grown used to hearing, "take a seat." The trouble is that in my mind very little gets done while one remains in that position. Maybe I am wrong.

In the fall of 2003 I attended a life-changing event in Toronto. My good friend Mohamed Gilao had a vision to rebuild a hospital in Mogadishu that had been destroyed in the early days of the Somali civil war. Mohamed invited me to a 'harambee' fundraiser. Committed to supporting this worthy cause, I promised that I would be there.

At the same time, a Kenyan diplomat stationed in Ottawa had a vision to return to his roots in Western Kenya. His dream was to help strengthen a rural community devastated by the HIV/AIDS pandemic. Before his retirement, he wanted to raise awareness of the plight of thousands of orphan children. When he heard about the fundraiser he eagerly accepted an invitation to attend.

I was late by one hour, and by the time I arrived I had missed some of the program. The guests were well into the first course of dinner. A quick glance around the room and there it was – one empty chair on the opposite side near the back. With no other options, I headed toward that space.

To my immediate left sat a very gracious and refined gentleman. He introduced himself as Malik Khaemba. For the past two decades he had served Kenya in the diplomatic corps. His posting to Canada would be his last. He had no idea that I was planning to travel to Kenya and I was unaware I would need his assistance to obtain a Kenya visa. How could we even begin to understand how our lives would later connect in such extraordinary ways?

I had recently retired from a career of thirty-three years as a teacher and school administrator. My post-retirement dream was to honour a promise made to a friend in the early 80's. Ron Ward had worked in Kenya as a teacher, humanitarian, medical development officer and disaster relief aid worker for nearly four decades. I was awed by his commitment and love for the Kenyan people. *'Ali D'Haeri'* was a name recognized in most areas of North East Province. Ron was a legend, a symbol of hope, and I wanted to see this amazing man in his adopted country.

As we ate, I shared with Malik my plan to spend three months in North East Province as a volunteer teacher at Garissa High School. While in Kenya I also hoped to visit schools across the country to conduct research on the impact of HIV/AIDS on the Kenyan school system. I described Garissa HS as an all boys school located on the main road leading east from the Tana River, right beside a mosque and close to the main hospital. The only medical clinic in Garissa specializing in the treatment of women and children was the Simaho Clinic. I was hoping to deliver much needed medical supplies and antibiotics to the nurses working there. To my delight, Malik told me that he would assist me to obtain a visa and special documents to clear the medical supplies through customs.

A few weeks later I visited Malik Khaemba in his office at the Kenya High Commission (Embassy) in Ottawa. During our conversation, we shared several cups of Kenya's finest 'masala' tea. It was there he said the words I will never forget, "When you are in Kenya you must visit the Kakamega Forest."

Kakamega? I had no idea it even existed. How would I ever get there from Garissa? If I had any spare time I would just as soon go on safari in the Masa Mara. What could I possibly do in Kakamega? Despite my doubts, something told me I needed to go.

During the last month I was in Kenya, I made good my promise to visit Malik's hometown. The seven-hour bus ride southwest from Garissa down the A3 past Mwingi and Thika to Nairobi was half the journey. The last 350 km took me past the incredible Rift Valley and the wildlife areas surrounding Lake Naivasha. Climbing to higher elevations, we saw sugar cane farms and tea plantations surrounding Kericho, Eldoret and Kaimosi. Finally after eight hours, the bus entered the outskirts of Kakamega.

As I stepped off the bus, I saw a man in a business suit approaching. Hillary Lukhafwa collected me and later that evening introduced me to Ben Udoto and Richard Masindet. Growing up with Malik, they had remained lifelong friends. Ben was a recently retired Headmaster of Kaimosi Teacher's College, Hillary was a senior officer with the Kenya Teacher's Service Commission, while Richard was an accountant whose expertise in establishing CES Kenya was invaluable.

I soon learned that this band of friends had a vision to do something in their community to support youth whose lives had been devastated by HIV/AIDS. I began to feel their heartbeat and was soon swept up by their passion to create a better life for the needy children around them. It was during our days together that the seeds of CES in Kenya and Canada were sown.

I had witnessed the tragedy of fragmented families, in particular children without any source of love and support. There was no escaping the sad images associated with the 1.2 million orphans living in Kenya. Never will I forget the scene where a carpenter had literally set up shop, building and selling coffins right beside the local infirmary; or the picture of orphans lining up to receive treatment from the community health nurse for 'jiggers', head lice, or the dreaded malaria. Many of these children had no place to call home, no place to sleep.

Could it be that I was in Kakamega for a reason? What I at first thought would be an educational travel experience had changed. Touched by the stories of the people I had come to know, I knew I would never be the same.

The 'empty chair' – was it fate that caused me to sit beside the man who invited me to visit a Kenyan rainforest? Could it be the circumstances that caused me to be late for the event; or was it the invitation by a friend to support a project in Somalia? Perhaps a promise made two decades earlier to visit a friend in Kenya was the start of the story that eventually made Community Education Services a reality.

In any event, I now see that 'empty chair' as a powerful symbol of personal transformation. It's the mystery of life, supernaturally sanctioned and not easily explained. It's the power that brings us to the realization that we are "our brother's keeper" and that our lives can only have meaning when we live in community with others. It's the stuff miracles are made of; it's the story behind CES Canada.

One thing is certain – 'the empty chair' has made all the difference.

by Michael Frederiksen

CHAPTER 2:

Meet the Patron

"Love is a Jewel"

Kenyan proverb

I Met a Man

I met a man who spoke of a land
sculptured by force of sun's extreme
rising high above Lake Victoria's deep
to the ancient hills of Nandi's dream.

I met a man who spoke of a land
where Stone of Ilesi silently cries,
calls upon heaven to embrace the humble,
precious orphans, angels in disguise.

I met a man who spoke of a land
of unparalleled beauty, nature's domain
where Kakamega's Forest in canopy green
sounds like heaven – abundance of rain.

I met a man who spoke of a land
given so freely by reason of birth
travelling the world he would always say
"there's nothing like Kakamega in all the earth."

Under the Acacia Tree Anthology
11/2011

Dedicated to Malik Khaemba, Patron CES Kenya
Friend and colleague in the fight against poverty and HIV/AIDS;
and, the reason CES Canada finds its heart in Kenya.

FROM AN INTERVIEW WITH MALIK KHAEMBA

CES stands for Community Education Services – the idea came up when I was about to retire in 2003. After working for almost thirty-one years in the public diplomatic service, it was in my mind that I wanted to give back to the community. I began to realize that I didn't want to go back home just to sit. I had gained a lot from the community and I needed to pay back. As the idea matured, I contacted my friends back home, people I grew up with. The concept was there before the name CES came to be. Consulting with my friends Ben and Hillary, I asked, "What can we do to pay or plough back to the community?"

Around that time, I met my friend Michael Frederiksen, currently the president of CES Canada. We met by chance at a fundraising event in Toronto, Canada. I shared with him this idea, which he picked up very quickly. Since I was not yet off duty and fully retired, we decided Michael should come to Kenya and meet my friends. Within a few months he arrived in Kakamega and it was agreed that our new initiative would be to support the community through education.

By the time Michael came back after three months in Kenya, we were already working on the document, describing the organization we wanted to build. We decided on the name, 'Community Education Services'. We were going to focus on serving the community from which we grew up.

By 2004 the program had already started. Organizing a '*harambee*' in Toronto, we raised enough funds for twelve scholarships. We agreed we were going to support the disadvantaged children in the community, meaning those children who had lost their parents. They were bright enough but did not have the funds to attend school.

The main thing we were focusing on was supporting those children affected and orphaned by HIV/AIDS. In 2004 we had twelve schools and twenty-four students to support. By the time I returned to Kenya in 2005 we had increased the number of schools to twenty-four, with two students on scholarship in each location. Forty-eight students, and now we had to find the resources to sponsor them. We had always made a promise that once brought into the program, that CES would support them until the completion of their secondary studies. We decided to concentrate on secondary school students because there were no other organizations in the county doing that.

Many elementary school graduates achieve very well; and so they receive a letter that allows them to register at a National secondary school like Alliance High School or Kamusinga High School. These are the big schools within our community; but, due to lack of finances many students are not able to attend. The only option left is a local community school. That is where CES Kenya picks them up for scholarship support.

Now I will explain to you on what basis we select the students who merit to register with the CES scholarship program. There must be a demonstrated financial need; either the parents are absent, or if one is present, there is severe economic hardship. Secondly, the child is bright, obtaining sufficient marks to move forward to high school. Thirdly, we are looking for disciplined students who have strong potential to become high achievers.

As a matter of policy, we agreed not to select the students ourselves. Our strategy was to partner with the principals of the schools; and so, we gave them the criteria to select the students and the numbers based on a limited budget.

Right from the word go, CES Kenya was an organization managed by a board of directors. The board designs the policies on which the program runs. We also have an executive board or secretariat as we like to call it. This is the small group that makes quick decisions, and eventually those decisions are ratified by the board and reflected in the minutes of the meeting. Board Chairman Ben Udoto is a founding member of CES Kenya. Without him CES would not be as efficient as it is. He is very passionate about the program and he has never missed a single sitting as chairman. He has been an excellent manager for CES. Then under him we have Hillary Lukhafwa as secretary who takes the minutes, and Treasurer Ibrahim Efumbi, who takes care of the finances and acts as our accountant.

I, Malik Khaemba, am the Patron. They gave me that title because I started the program and double up as a Chief Executive Officer. I do most of the office communications and correspondence. Supported by Executive Office Manager Sarah Nabongo, together we do most of the administrative work. We have Directors meetings at least four times per year and more as needs arise. I'm proud to say that we have been doing this since 2004. After my retirement I came straight to Kakamega and we put everything in motion. We have never looked back since that time.

FROM DIPLOMAT TO HUMANITARIAN

by John Guthrie, CES Volunteer to Kenya

"We have started something that is difficult to stop." These were the words that Malik Khaemba spoke to me on July 14, 2011. He was of course referring to the good works of Community Education Services Kenya. He was also acknowledging the partnership with Canadians that has provided a way for hundreds of students to go to school in the Kakamega District of Western County.

In telling me how CES Kenya came to be, Malik became animated. He reminded me of the story of 'the empty chair' where in 2003 some amazing circumstances brought he and Michael Frederiksen together. He talked about his special friendship with Chairman Ben (Udoto) from the time they met in secondary school.

Friendship is a key theme throughout our talk. Patron Malik remembers his Canadian friends very fondly. He talks of how, as a Kenyan diplomat, he enjoyed immensely the people he met in Canada between 2000 and 2005. Of all his international postings, Canada was where he says he received the warmest welcome.

Malik is proud of the fact that his family was able to support his attendance at school: "I was never kept home from school for lack of fees." And yet, he understands the situation that hundreds of thousands of children find themselves in. Now he makes it his life's mission to do something about helping as many of them as possible.

Pride is evident throughout his description of his life. I came to realize that the pride of this Kenyan elder is not the pride that some think of as a deadly sin. He is proud of his diplomatic service for his country. He opened the mission in Abu Dhabi and served in Brussels before coming to Ottawa, Canada. Malik was commended and recognized for his diplomatic skills, receiving the Head of State Commendation (Hsc).

Despite his return to his homeland, he is very happy that his three eldest children are now living in Canada. Yet, for himself, he had a feeling that he would never be anything other than Kenyan. It was vital for him to renew his relationship with his people, and return to Kenya for the next step in his life after diplomatic service.

I sensed a man with deep compassion for others. Even before his retirement, Malik knew that his heart was set on returning to Kenya to devote his life to humanitarian outreach. His desire to provide hope through education, to alleviate poverty and to fight the ravages of HIV/AIDS was strong and determined. Since then he has been the driving force in Kakamega County to coordinate and provide nearly 3500 education scholarships for needy students. He has worked to create a strong base for education and community support in his home area and beyond.

In addition, Malik Khaemba was appointed to a government organized committee to lay the groundwork for the 2009 Kenya Constitution. His skills in strategic planning and defining the elements of electoral reform have been recognized. In 2010 Malik Khaemba was asked to be a district leader (Malava/Lurambi), training others to communicate to their constituencies the basic tenants of the new Kenya Constitution. Over a five-month period he worked tirelessly to help people understand and educate them to the realities of their new civic responsibilities.

Malik is passionate about community service. He has assembled an exceptional group of Board Directors that assist him in the work of providing hope through education. The results are clear with a history of CES grads attending college and university and a number employed as educators and medical professionals.

Patron Malik feels a strong bond with his Canadian friends. He considers the life in Canada to be easier compared to his homeland, notwithstanding the harsh winter weather. Nonetheless, he is very appreciative of the visits that are made by seventy Canadians volunteers who have helped to create strong relationships and have worked on key community projects.

Malik says that we (CES) are making his community better and stronger. "CES Kenya is grateful for the special partnership with CES Canada that promotes a better future for Kenyan youth." He speaks proudly of graduates like Mary Kandia and Benjamin Wafula: "If it were not for CES, Mary would not be attending university and Benjamin would not be employed as a teacher."

As Patron Malik goes, so goes CES in Kenya. He is the backbone of CES, our eyes and ears "on the ground", watching over all that has been created in rural western Kenya. As we part, Malik Khaemba leaves me with another gem to consider: "We must be prepared to meet the challenges that we ourselves have created."

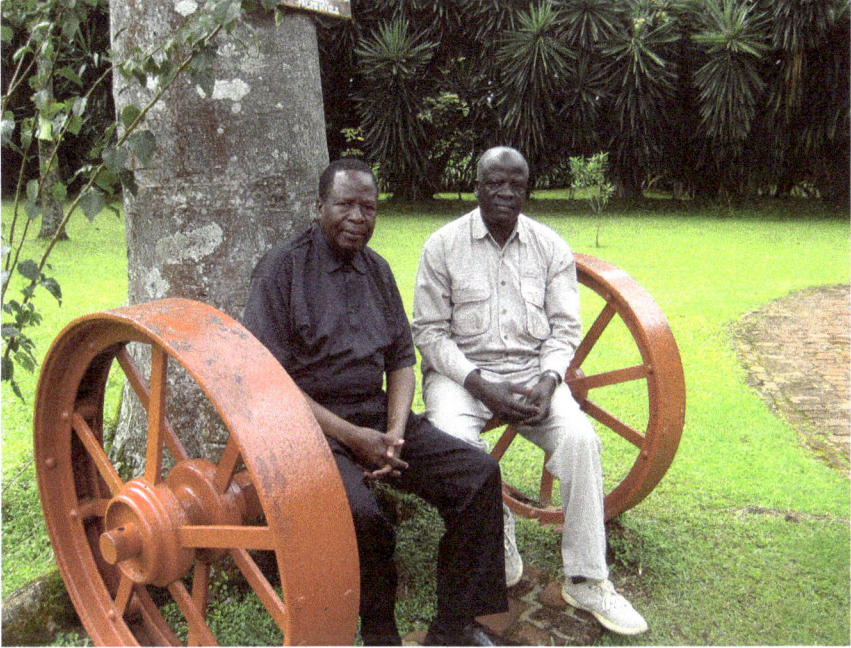

Bonds of friendship established in their youth helped to create a mutual desire to give back to their community. Here, Malik Khaemba (left), Patron of CES Kenya and Ben Udoto, Chairman of CES Kenya share memories. The seeds of CES were planted here at Rondo Retreat — in the heart of the Kakamega Forest.

CES Canada President Michael Frederiksen celebrates the 10th Anniversary of CES in Kenya with a group of students from Kakamega Muslim Secondary School.

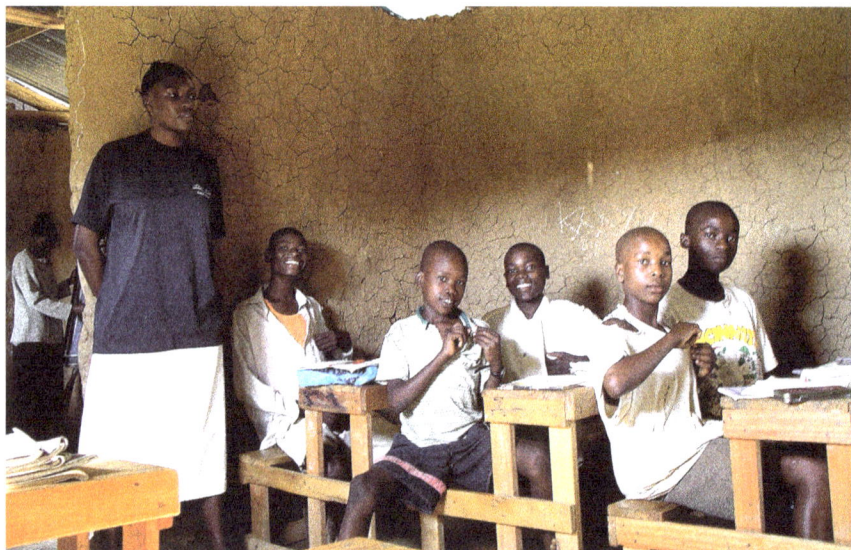

Informal schools exist without state funding, providing basic literacy and numeracy skills for many orphaned youth in Kenya. Seated in the back row beside his teacher is seventeen year-old Patrick Shisiali. The blue bag on his desk contains all he owns in life. This scene was the inspiration that started a charity to provide education scholarships, later to be known as CES Canada.

Felistas Barasa, former Principal of Namirama Girls Secondary School encourages her CES graduating students. Mdme Barasa has been a long-time friend and supporter of CES, an inspirational school leader, admired by her students.

CHAPTER 3:

Why Kakamega?

"Go East or West, but home is the best"

Kenyan proverb

ROAD TO RONDO

Everywhere you go in Kakamega County, whether by day or night, the roads are crowded with people walking and carrying things. Men lead their animals by a thick rope and boys carry sticks to beat and prod goats and unruly donkeys into moving in the right direction. Women bent double under the weight of firewood, and children carrying water from a nearby stream somehow carry on. These are the ones who except while sleeping, never experience relief from their labours.

Motor bikes and bicycles with huge loads weave in and out of traffic. Bicycle taxis known as *boda bodas* carrying passengers and three wheeled *tuk-tuks* fill the roadways. *Matatus* or mini buses with signs like 'God is Able' and 'Answered Prayer' plastered on the back window pick up passengers. *Pikipiki* motorcycles wait at street corners to collect the ones brave enough to get on them. It is common to see four persons hanging on to the driver. On the main roads there are lots of old lorries that frequently break down. Except for expensive SUV's, most cars are old and beaten up; many are obtained from the Middle East as reconditioned vehicles.

Markets, kiosks, stalls and shops line the roads leading out of town. The whole scene can best be described as purposeful pandemonium.

Kakamega has a wonderful climate with rich red clay soil for growing. The famous Kakamega Forest is the only rainforest in Kenya, an eco-tourism destination. Subsistence farming is how most people support themselves. A major societal problem is land ownership. In Kenya the land is subdivided between the male sons in the family. Cultivation has spread as far as it can, and now the other sons just have to go off and find jobs in the city. There is not enough land for all families to continue in their traditional ways.

Up until recently, land could not be owned by a daughter in the family. Girls had no choice but to get married and live with the husband and his family. As a result, education has become more important, most often seen as the only way out of a life of poverty.

The typical homestead or *shamba* is a rectangular 200 sq ft hut with walls of mud brick and a roof of corrugated iron. There are a few of the old thatched round huts left; usually these are used for cooking or storage. Whatever land is available is used to grow crops of maize, beans and grain and to raise a few goats and chickens.

Towns and villages are full of bustle and enterprise. People are working hard with a few simple tools making furniture, steel windows, and repairing anything broken. Others sell a few bananas, potatoes, fruits or roasted maize. Some women cook "chapati" or flat bread over a small container stoked with embers of charcoal. Young children sell pieces of sugar cane or roasted maize. In the midst of all this confusion, chickens, goats and cows roam about freely. Villagers grow most of what they need. To buy clothes, paraffin, salt, flour etc. they will sell a few bananas, sugar cane, firewood, whatever they can find. When cash is scarce, bartering is common.

A major cash crop is sugar cane. The Mumias sugar factory located near Kakamega is a big local employer. There are also tea co-ops where women deliver large baskets filled with freshly picked tea. Tea in Kenya is grown at 2000 metres above sea level where the soil conditions for growing and the prevailing winds and rain patterns are ideal for producing high quality tea. Tropical climates and red volcanic soils rich in nutrients give Kenya tea a unique body and flavour.

From Kakamega, the road to Rondo stretches for miles. Kiosks line the tarmac as we first pass the Golf Hotel, then the Kakamega General Hospital. Bars, butcheries, fruit and vegetable stands, furniture and steel gate manufacturers and outdoor hair salons compete for business. It is only 7:00 AM and the marketplace has been active for the past two hours. A lifetime of hustling, that's what it takes to survive in Kenya.

Adjacent to the hospital entrance lies a stack of ready-made wooden coffins, some so tiny only a small child could fit. An entrepreneur has figured out that locating here will optimize his earnings. HIV/AIDS continues its relentless assault on western Kenya. Yet there is progress with foundations built for a new teaching referral hospital.

Around the bend on the right we see the newly constructed green and white iron gates of Bishop Sulumeti Girls HS. Since 2008 CES has provided secondary scholarships here. Other infrastructure projects include the Oasis of Learning Library and a fully operational two-acre zero graze dairy farm.

Straight ahead is Shieywe SS, the second CES associated school we pass. Located at the edge of the Kakamega Forest, our 'songbird school' is continuously serenaded by the delightful sounds of over eighty bird species. Children in school uniform, women carrying bananas and vegetables to market, others with huge loads of sticks and wood branches balanced on their heads form a steady stream of humanity walking on either side of the road. In Kenya people walk, some for hundreds of kilometres at a stretch.

Matatu, *pikipiki* and *boda boda* operators compete to collect the 50 shillings needed for a ride to town. Tethered goats and chickens scrounge for whatever food and scraps are available. Somewhere in all this confusion there's a six-year-old kid chewing on a piece of sugar cane. Wearing a tattered shirt and walking barefoot, the image tells a tragic story of neglect. He bears all the signs of alcohol poisoning - loss of hair, glazed eyes and an unsteady walk. Without a school uniform or a pair of shoes he will never attend school. He and hundreds like him live on the edge of survival.

Crossing the Yala River, the pavement changes to a road full of potholes littered with rocks the size of a large fist. Our Toyota SUV with its 20-inch double tread tires takes the same abuse as we do. Affectionately known as the 'Kenyan massage', the journey to Rondo Retreat is designed to toughen us up.

At Shinyalu Town we turn south and from here the road turns a shiny reddish brown colour. Shiny for its clay content, and red for the iron in the ground. Early morning rainfall creates a high gloss look akin to a fresh coat of paint. On the left is Lugala Friends Church. This thriving congregation of Quakers has been in the area for over a century. In nearby Kaimosi, the Society of Friends built a teacher training facility. Hundreds of schools and hospitals were opened throughout East Africa in the early 20th century by Quaker missionaries from England.

We pass groups of girls laughing and skipping their way to school. They look so smart in their brown and cream coloured school uniforms. Facing a relentless pressure to succeed, the hopes of their entire family rests on how well each girl achieves. Lirhanda Girls HS is a perennial winner at national dramatic arts festivals. Their extraordinary production on the theme of child labour won the 2016 national gold award. As we pass by the school gates, we enjoy the familiar shout out 'mzungu'. Lirhanda Girls is the last CES school we pass on route to Rondo Retreat.

A barricade appears ahead and we are forced to stop at a check point. Here a soldier armed with an AK-47 guards the official entrance to the forest. A spike strip with its collection of three inch long metal barbs straddles the roadway. Either we stop or the tires on our vehicle will be punctured. We do the right thing.

A barrage of questions, like what is our business and how long will be our visit to the forest are not as important as the real concern. The main reason for this stop is to make it clear that it is illegal to cut or collect wood in the Kakamega Forest. Sadly, that can be nullified by a 100-bob bribe. Women routinely walk the ten kilometres from Shinyalu to collect firewood and then take it back to their home to boil water and cook food. They have no concept that once the forest disappears they will be displaced, their very livelihood, agriculture and source of food lost. They live in the immediate with day to day survival their only reality.

We now travel under an incredible canopy of foliage. Light filters through branches, bouncing off leaves of century old trees. Driving through a kaleidoscope of exciting shapes and colours we finally arrive. On our right are the gates of Rondo Retreat, entrance to 'paradise'.

I recall my first visit to Rondo in March 2004. A dozen excursions later, the grounds remain unchanged, as if in a time warp. This magical place has become an annual pilgrimage not to be missed. Here friendships blossom and new beginnings take place. It is an escape from the real world of rural Kenya. Therapeutic and good for the soul, the brutality of life disappears in the light of a gentler world.

Rondo is a Christian retreat centre built by the Presbyterian Church in the mid 1960's, as a retreat for retired ministers. For a brief period in the 70's it was also an orphanage. Starting with the rolling lawns and flowerbeds of Rondo's upper garden, one can walk through the dappled light to the fish pond and a lower garden. There are numerous trails leading into the forest. A 40-minute hike leads to Lirhanda Hill. It rises above the forest canopy with stunning vistas of the forest and surrounding countryside.

Trees of tremendous height, great girth and massive buttresses are draped with hanging lianas. A mix of lowland and highland flora and fauna and flowers including sixty kinds of orchids make this area an environmental delight. Nearly four hundred species of birds and representatives of every African family of butterflies sustain biology tourism at the Kakamega Forest.

The homestead consists of the main house of clapboard and colonial era corrugated iron, and five cottages in the same old style, all decorated using antique prints, local paintings, crafts and fabrics. The cuisine is excellent. English breakfasts, midday lunches, and candlelit dinners are served in a cozy dining room. Tea can be taken in the sitting room, on the main verandah, or on the lawn. A chapel built on the edge of the garden is next to the forest. Set apart from the other houses it is ideal for solitude, individual prayer and meditation. Life at Rondo is uncomplicated, a place of refreshing, healing; that thin space between heaven and earth where the heart is at peace and the soul at rest.

Warm winds from west Africa collect moisture from Lake Victoria some seventy kilometres to the east. The Nandi Hills create the catch basin where the rains fall on a 3000 sq km area known as Kakamega Forest, a gift for the Luhya people.

Malik Khaemba first introduced me to this place. I have never forgotten his words, "When in Kenya you must visit Kakamega Forest." And so Rondo symbolizes the very beginnings of CES in Kenya where our first planning session took place. It took more than one meeting at Rondo to form a plan of action. In fact it did not happen until after I returned to Canada. But the seeds of CES Canada were sown at Rondo Retreat Centre. The venture became more clear after I returned to Canada; and in the most unlikely location, Newfoundland.

A six week stay in Canada's most eastern province was just perfect to recuperate after extensive surgery. As I grew stronger and more fit, Linda and I would take long walks around Peace Cove Bay to Trinity East. We hiked the Skerwink Trail to see the whales as they migrated south. Getting to know the locals brought me a huge appreciation for life and what it meant to truly be alive. It was also a time to reflect on my experience in Kenya. It was during these days in Newfoundland that the vision of CES Canada was birthed.

Malik returned to Kenya in 2005. CES had already begun to support students in their education. By 2006 we celebrated our first graduate, Benjamin Wafula. He would later become the first Chairman of the CES Alumni. After fifteen years operating in Kakamega County, over 3500 secondary and post secondary scholarships have been made available to students in forty-five school communities.

The challenges have been huge and at times our mission to Kenya has been tough. It has not been easy, and seeing people suffer has taken its toll on many of us – burnout, stress and an inescapable emotional fallout.

Rondo has for me become the antidote, a reminder of humble beginnings, a hiatus from the stress of dealing with real life challenges. Most importantly, it's a place to renew friendships and spend a day appreciating our incredible Kenyan associates.

Time is not always measured in seconds and minutes. At Rondo it can be said that a day spent in paradise is better than a year anywhere else. If that's true, then I have spent a dozen years in paradise. And that is more than most will experience in a lifetime.

by Michael Frederiksen

CHAPTER 4:
The Wall

"Truth is Stronger than Weapons"

Kenyan proverb

Most people who visit Africa will face it. When it happens, your world stands still. You are left with your emotions right out there; raw, nothing hidden. The Wall will break your heart, but not your spirit. It will move you to the core of your being. You will never be the same.

The Wall forces us to see life more clearly. It exposes us to the truth. It hurts. To hit the Wall is to be broken. Only the power of love can bring healing; but even then, scars will remain. The Wall opens the eyes of the soul to a new reality, the beauty and the pathos of a fellow human being's story.

We normally engage people on the surface level. We only understand and hear a fraction of their story. The Wall forces us below the surface, behind the veneer to see what is really happening.

In 2004 I met Marie McKay (1938-2015), a retired Canadian nurse who volunteered most recently with KEEF (Kenya Education Endowment Fund). Previously in Kenya, I had seen poverty but had not yet internalized what that meant to the one living in it. I had just come from North-East Kenya in a desert region where water for washing, hygiene and personal needs was rationed at two litres per day. That I could handle.

During my days in Kakamega, Marie took me to a non-formal school, a one room corrugated tin covered mud dwelling without windows or a door. These schools are designed to teach the basics of numeracy and literacy only. I met Francis Omondi, teacher of twelve boys age 8-18 years. I observed her students as she taught them the basics of math and English communications. They were so happy to receive the Canadian flag pins I had brought for them. In the corner sat Patrick Shisiali, oldest in the class. On his desk was a small blue plastic bag; and when I enquired, was told all his possessions and everything he owned was in that bag.

Teachers routinely travelled the remote countryside to identify young people who were not in school. They had found Patrick up a tree sleeping for protection against wild animals at night. When he was asked to attend school, he said he could not because he had no shoes. In fact he had never owned a pair of shoes.

Patrick's story was too much for me to handle. I left the mud hut with its cracked walls, stepped outside and found a quiet place. I cried for Patrick, sobbing like one who had lost something dear and precious. I was broken and totally destroyed emotionally. I felt the hand of Marie on my shoulder. She said in a quiet voice, "It's OK, we all go through it." I had just hit the Wall and it had brought me to my knees. I had just witnessed and felt the pain of another. It was at that moment I knew I had to do something.

HIV/AIDS is a fierce enemy that leaves in its wake orphans and widows. The most vulnerable are young women and children. UNICEF refers to these children as "excluded and invisible, living in the shadows." Rather than a time of joy, growth and learning, childhood for them has become a shadow land of pain, suffering and despair.

These extraordinary youth face poverty and adversity each day. Little in life has been prepared for them; yet their outlook on life remains one of joy and celebration. Why are they so happy? What gives them hope? How can they succeed in the face of such adversity?

Agnes is one of the 'Orphan Kids of Kakamega' who used to dream of a secondary school education. Now she has been given new hope. Against huge odds she has won the lottery of life, a chance to attend secondary school. One would think that in Kenya that would be a non-negotiable right. Not so. In January 2003, President Mwai Kibaki introduced a free primary education initiative, giving a million children the chance to attend school. There were however no additional teachers hired and few resources to handle this latest group of learners.

Agnes was swept up in this wave of excitement as children showed up to attend her local school. She enrolled in Standard Three, but it was not until 2011 some eight years later, that she graduated from Primary School. A very bright girl, she stood first in her class. Her father died before she could remember his face, and over the years her mother struggled alone to raise six children. Being the third-born and eldest girl, Agnes often had to stay home to fetch water, do chores and care for younger siblings. In 2006 her mother became ill from a cholera epidemic and Agnes was forced to remain home to run the household. An entire year of schooling was lost. By the time the disease had run its course, hundreds of families were left parentless, and many children had died. Fortunately, Agnes' mother survived; however, she was too weak to work in the fields as a labourer or as a hired house help. In all, it took her eleven years to complete her Standard 8.

Now she was ready for secondary school. She wanted so badly to attend at Bukhakunga SS. It was clear however, that Agnes could not pay the school fees. On January 2012, while others wore new uniforms and shoes for their first day in Form 1, she remained home. Agnes felt that life had already passed her by. She did not know that her primary school principal was working on a plan for her.

Other village girls were unable to attend school and some as young as age fourteen were being married, often to men three times their age. Agnes had a friend from school who at age 15 was married with one child, and another soon to be born. Another had disappeared overnight. No one talked about it, but it was rumoured that a relative had taken her to Nairobi to become a servant girl to a wealthy family.

Agnes managed to gain entrance to Secondary School on the strength of her high marks. Later in the first Term of Form 1, she heard she was being recommended for a CES scholarship. All she needed was a certified document signed by the chief of her area that she was a partial orphan. She already had her mother's blessing.

During an official school visit in September 2014 I met Agnes. We were following up on our CES sponsored students to get a picture of how they were doing in school. The entrance to her school was guarded by a gate, typical of all Kenyan schools. The motto of St Patrick's Bukhakunga SS, 'Keen to Succeed', was clearly written on the wall. First, we greeted the watchman, signing his logbook. Inside the compound there was evidence of recent tree planting. Flowering bushes, deep purple morning glory and a variety of hibiscus flowers were in full bloom. In the centre of the school quad area flew the Kenyan flag. Bukhakunga SS was established in 1975 as a 'Harambee School', meaning it was built by the will and resources of the local community and sponsored by the Catholic Diocese of Kakamega. It became a government school in 1989.

Since 2005 this school has partnered with CES Kenya to provide scholarships for orphaned youth. Some of our CES sponsored students had recently participated at the national level in a "choral verses" competition during the 2013 Kenya Secondary School Music Festival. Principal Ferdinand Musi proudly displayed the trophies that lined a cabinet to the side of his office desk. Bukhakunga SS had a population of 480, where the ratio of boys to girls was 2:1. The Principal responded to my concern with, "In Kenya things are slowly changing."

Bukhakunga SS is well known in the area for its Science programs. Despite the fact it has no library or internet facility or even a science lab, the school placed first in the County in senior Chemistry, Biology and Physics. An enterprising teacher made arrangements with Masinde Muliro University of Science and Technology for his students to use the science lab facilities on weekends, all on his own time and without compensation.

The school was appreciated for another reason. Its borehole, a source of clean water was open to villagers and neighbouring homes. Bukhakunga SS was better off than many surrounding schools that operated without electricity, water or proper latrines. Students in these rural schools routinely took time from their daytime studies to walk up to two kilometres to fetch water from a nearby river. Classrooms were run down and crowded with three students seated at each desk. I remember in the early years of our work talking to a Form 2 Geography class on the topic of Canada's St Lawrence Seaway. To my surprise, they were learning about the engineering and building of the Welland Canal in Ontario, Canada. One hundred students were eager to learn in a small classroom built for forty, standing room only.

Dressed in dark blue school uniforms, our students were waiting for us at the gate, their beautiful smiles a great welcome after a hot, dusty and bumpy one-hour drive from our home base in Kakamega. But first the traditional "sign in" procedure at the main office and then warm soda and biscuits, Kenyan hospitality at its finest. There is a record of each time in the past fifteen years I have visited at Bukhakunga.

One of the things I love the most about visits to our schools is meeting the students. Curious about what Kenyans know about Canada I asked the same question, "What do you know about Canada?" One indicated that Canada had been friendly to Kenya. I was surprised at one response, "How is Saskatchewan?" Another added that he felt Canada had provided spiritual influence. Agnes told us that Canada had provided a home for Kenyans. I told her that was true, that over 10,000 Kenyan born were living in the Province of Ontario.

"Please send my appreciation to Canada and all those who support Kenyan students through CES. I didn't ever think I would attend a secondary school. I never thought it was possible." Her humble and dignified approach was evident. Mature and wise for her years, I knew this young woman had leadership potential.

Agnes enjoyed senior status in Form 4. She was also the head girls prefect. As we talked and toured the school, I noticed several holes in her school sweater. She was particularly interested in showing us the dormitory buildings. With several cracks in the walls and a few broken windows, it became clear this was no safe haven against the deadly malaria-bearing mosquito.

With that in mind I asked, "Agnes, what would be the most important thing CES could for students at Bukhakunga?" I recalled how another student had responded to the same question. What he wished for most was a bar of soap to keep clean and take away the body odour. Agnes spoke up, "The keys to good health are drinking clean water, washing hands with soap and sleeping under a net. Our students need nets," she said.

The cost for a treated anti-malaria mosquito net is CDN$8. Such a small investment to save a life. Agnes' vision was for all our students to have a net to sleep under. Ever since her appeal, students entering the CES scholarship program receive a net. And just in case you were wondering, we purchased two brand new sweaters so that she could continue to lead the girls with the dignity required of a Head Prefect.

'Hitting the Wall' – how does that relate to Agnes? The concept here is in reverse. It's not *mzungu* who has reacted; on the contrary, it's a young Kenyan girl who has experienced enough hardship and wants to do something about it. It took a lot of courage for Agnes to even approach me, let alone present her plea on behalf of herself and others. The Wall for her was the ever present and deadly mosquito – and she was just plain tired of it.

Kenyans will move forward as they take ownership and seek solutions to the challenges they face. Kenya needs more young people like Agnes to speak up and demand the rights and freedoms afforded to those with greater means and privilege. Kenyans are very patient and put up with a lot. Their hope lies in what may happen tomorrow, and not what is currently the case. What really needs to happen is for this generation of youth to stand for what is right, to have a voice and demand to be treated fairly.

The Wall must come down, enough is enough! I am confident in Agnes and hundreds of other CES Alumni to do their part to bring down that Wall of injustice, a barrier that prohibits access to basic health care and education. Slowly but surely - '*kidogo kidogo*', changes are happening.

by Michael Frederiksen

Rural Education

I am a child like you once were
for the mirror tells the story
opens up a world of learning
Education within our locality
a potential life enhancing light.

Favourable environmental conditions
cheaper means of acquiring knowledge
create an exhilaration of learning
drawing us towards our fantastic dreams
to be great doctors and engineers.

Underscored in Vision 2030
the role of education stands paramount
providing a road map for development
in economic, social and political aspects
lighting up darkened rural communities.

The intrinsic value of education unseen
our schools devoid of learning equipment
financial problems plaguing our hearts
hampering our education throughout our lives
withering our fortunes, our hopes in vain.

The few rural strugglers
who rise above their rural origin
often shy away from addressing experiences
of rural primitivity and ignorance
cutting links with the less fortunate
thus maintaining the obnoxious gap
that separates urban from rural.

Most dreaded aspects of rural setting
includes envy and abject corruption
suppression and oppression by the richer
demeaning any encouragement and inspiration
save for Khaemba and Udoto
and CES Board members
who have served far above the rest.

Pity the poor rural region
with no institutions for higher learning
inaccessible transport and communication networks
little government sponsorship in place
and not forgetting exposure to the modern world
ever leads us to brain drain.

Not narrowed to intellectual development
education is acquisition and application
of knowledge for positive gain
my appeal is to the education sector
to design a method of our equal rescue
ensuring public universities and tertiary colleges
building branches in rural areas.

By Sheila Nasindu - CES Grad (2009)
10/2011

Part II

Unacceptable Reality

CHAPTER 5:

Iron Girl

"Good things come to those who persevere"

Kenyan proverb

by Patricia Nyanchama Makori, Director, CES Kenya
Principal CESCED (School of Continuing Education)

Kisii County is characterized by hilly topography with several ridges and lush valleys. Located in the Rift Valley, Kisii is the main urban and commercial centre in the Gusii Highlands and the South Nyanza region of Kenya. It is here that Kanana ("little one") is born and raised as a child.

Kanana is eleven years old. She is the eldest of eight children, four boys and four girls. Her parents, like most people in Kenya, have no reliable jobs. They do casual work to make ends meet. There is never enough to go around. From the age of eight, Kanana learned how to cook, and she soon had the responsibility to prepare food for her younger siblings. Kanana's goal is to become a lawyer. The road ahead will not be easy.

"I once witnessed my school desk-mate being sexually abused by a neighbour. I had to appear in Court to account for what happened. I watched the female lawyer and knew that fighting for justice was what I wanted to do. I know my parents cannot raise my school fees, but I will do anything to change our situation."

As the firstborn girl-child, Kanana is expected to cook, look after her younger siblings and tend to the garden. She has never 'stolen an eye' (travelled) into even a small town. She comes from the bush. That is how the rich describe children living under poverty. Her home is fenced with poisonous thorns. There is no electricity, only an empty tin lamp with no paraffin. It remains standing in a dark corner in her grass thatched house. When the sky is clear, she is able to do homework under the moonlight outside their house. Her thighs have become a working table.

The only staple food she knows is *ugali* (a thick cornmeal porridge) and *sukuma wiki* (the name means 'to stretch the week') made of collard greens, a low-cost local vegetable; boiled in water and salt. It's only on Christmas day when her family can afford rice and beef. At 6 o'clock news time there is no television, radio, and no computer. When others in her class talk about movies, computer games, rib cracking jokes and stories heard from radio, Kanana wonders what they are talking about. They silence her with, "Aha! You're from the bush. Don't engage us with endless questions. Is this a police station where you interrogate people or are you a police woman? Shut up and go ask your mum such simple questions that even your grandma can answer without thinking."

Kanana has no idea what an alarm clock looks like. Her internal clock wakes her up most days and once in a while she is woken up by her mother or by a neighbour's rooster crow. This obedient girl must complete morning duties before going to school. She carries ripe bananas in a basket on her head, walking to market six kilometres each way. Back home, on a good day she takes a breakfast of black tea and then asks her skeleton legs to carry her to school.

Many days she is late for school. Her teachers call her 'notorious late comer'. To add to this humility, other duties await her. These include cleaning the school teachers' latrines and collecting rubbish. After the morning assembly she happens to be among those sent away from school or punished from time to time because she has no school uniform or has not paid school fees. In shame Kanana is forced to walk five kilometres barefoot along the red clay dusty road that brings her home. In her right hand she carries books and in her left some pieces of collected firewood.

She knows when she gets home she will have to walk another four kilometres to fetch water.

Somehow she is able to stay at the top of her class despite a world that does not care she even exists. Kanana has no time to play as the weekend comes knocking. Unlike her friends, she is set to go hawking ground nuts, sugar cane, guavas and whatever is available. She hopes no one will see her weeding and harvesting maize at their rich neighbour's shamba (garden). A few shillings will be raised to help pay some of her school fees. Her mother works as a house help close by. That means Kanana is responsible for carrying her younger sister on her back while she works.

Darkness tiptoes in. It is time for birds to sing their lullaby songs sending their ancestors to bed. Kanana listens to their sweet melodies as she cooks on three stones. After the arrival of her mother they sit around the fire to warm themselves. A meal is not a guarantee. On a bad day Kanana goes to bed on an empty stomach; she foregoes food so that her mother can get milk to breast feed their newborn baby. She sacrifices so her younger brothers and sister can eat the little that is available. Finally after nine o'clock it is time to retire. Everyone sleeps together on tattered rugs spread over the dirt floor. Sounds of the night include the shouts of drunkards as they stagger home after another drinking spree. Kanana will be the first one to rise the next morning.

Kanana deserves more. She is strong and courageous. She has never had a childhood and has never known what it feels like to be tucked into bed. She does not worry about sleeping at night without a mosquito net. Malaria has struck many times, for her it is a part of life. What about her dreams, are they too soon to be crushed? The scourge of HIV/AIDS, will it destroy a promising young life? Will poverty take its toll and keep Kanana from reaching her education goals? Will she be discarded as trash or will she rise above it all to create a future for herself. Something tells me she will.

After all, they don't call her "Iron Girl" without good reason.

Mzungu says: 'Iron Girl' describes the indomitable spirit of the girl-child in Kenya who when given a chance to attend school show an inner strength, like iron it will not bend.

THE DAY THEY TOOK ME IN

by Truphosa A. Omukangu, Form 2, Namundera SS
Winner of 2012 CES Kenya Literary Award

Is this the life I was made to have? Why did God bring me into a world of distress? Every morning I am sent home and told to bring back school fees. I was not given time to stay at school for a single minute. If money for school fees were a plant, I would have planted, reaped and taken it to school so that my education could run smoothly.

In our family of eight children, I was the only girl to reach Standard Four. Due to lack of school fees and the difficult life we had undergone, I almost gave up hope of finishing school. My poor parents struggled tooth and nail but their efforts were still in vain. In my schooling, I had no uniform or stationery. I used to collect papers and borrowed some from friends, glued them together and used them as a book. One friend gave me her old uniform. It looked like a rainbow due to different rags perched on it to close the gaps.

Worse still, there rose a conflict between my father and mother. At first I thought it was going to cease but it ended in separation. My father decided to sell half an acre, the only land we had. He married another wife and like a piece of wood thrown and discarded in the middle of a stormy ocean, we were left homeless.

My primary school education came to a sudden halt. We had no food, shelter or clothing. With no land to cultivate, we could only beg our neighbours for flour, potatoes and paraffin. I wished the ground to open up and swallow me alive. My wishes played hide and seek with my mind. I decided to go to Mrs Everlyne Wanga, my mother's best friend. I would take care of her children and do other house chores so I could earn five shillings to take to school. Life was more difficult there. I worked without food. Sometimes I ate the remains off her plate. I persevered because I wanted an education.

I used to work to pay for my primary school fees. I went to school at the end of term examinations and even though I was a frequent absentee I scored in the top ten. In Standard Eight my hope of sitting for the Kenya Certificate of Primary Education was almost buried. There was a lot of money to be paid and food such as maize to be brought to school. My friends had left me saying, "We are fed up with your borrowing, buy your own."

By good luck Principal John Keya felt touched by my suffering and paid the exam registration fee. I thanked the Creator. I came to realize the truth of the saying that God never forsakes his people. I struggled as much as I could to ensure that no one overtook me in performance.

"Let us see what she will get. She has wasted a lot of money going to school instead of getting married like her sisters and having children. Even if she passes the examination, what secondary school will take her in?" When the results were released, I did not believe what I saw. I was first, with 354 marks.

I was invited to join Mukumu Girls' High School but I did not go. I had my heart set on it, but the school fees were too high. And so I joined Namundera Mixed SS late towards the end of the first term. I emerged as the second best student. I impressed my teachers so much that it was proposed I would benefit from a CES scholarship.

When I arrived the next day I was so happy. I received a pink and blue uniform, new shoes, text and exercise books and a good bag. That was the happiest day of my life, the day they took me in. This was the day of rejoicing, for now I had become a CES student. Now I can go about my day without hurrying or hesitating. I am working hard towards my vision of becoming a doctor. If it was the darkness that engulfed my ways, it was now CES shining brightly to light the way.

Poverty, Enemy of the People

Poverty, who are you?
where do you come from?
if you want a cow, come own it
leave me alone.

Once you entered there was no food
shelter ran away, education withered
if you want my tatters come take them
leave me alone.

Where you pass there is stealing
where you perch you cause laughter
where you stay, you sire street children
if you want my shoes come take them
leave me alone.

I will shake you shamelessly
through the CES organization
CES, light my way
give me power and strength
to end poverty, enemy of the people
buried in an endless, bottomless pit
I am not alone

Truphosa A. Omukangu
09/2012

Because I am a Girl

I collect water, firewood and scraps of burlap and cloth
for me there is never a break;
I watch my brothers go to school while I stay home
for me it may be too late;
I eat if there's still food left when everyone else is done,
for me stomach ulcers and hunger pangs are normal;
I know what it is like to be among the poorest of the poor

Because I am a Girl
I am the soul of my community,
I will sing a song of hope and joy,
I will impart wisdom to the next generation,
I will lift my family out of poverty, I will give all that I am
…and, if you invest in me, I will never let you down.

Because I am a Girl

Under the Acacia Tree Anthology
06/2010

Mzungu says: 'Because I am a Girl' was written in response to a CES-sponsored student whose gentle spirit and courageous approach to life has been extraordinary. After graduating in 2011, Mary Kandia volunteered as a teacher assistant to mentor younger CES-sponsored students at her own Namundera SS. She represents the hopes and dreams of many girls unable to attend school. Mary is indeed the 'soul of her community', and her character and strong heart are mirrored in this poem.

CHAPTER 6: SCOURGE OF HIV/AIDS

"War has no eyes"

Kenyan proverb

Mzungu says: There are all kinds of data and information available on the internet along with an abundance of research initiatives on the topic of HIV/Aids. Kenya suffers deeply as 1.2 million orphans under the age of 18 years are affected by the Aids pandemic. Rather than concentrate on facts and numbers, it is poetry in this chapter that focuses on the affective and emotional side of a society decimated by Aids.

The Scourge

When death came
and took away our parents
we were left with no hope
wondering who could be next in line
friends, relatives abandoned us
now we are living on garbage food.

We used to laugh at them
today it is us
tomorrow it might be you
who will sing for us a comforting song?

Penina Mukami, Kamenu PS Thika
02/2004

Under the Mpundu Tree

Mzungu says: HIV/AIDS is a topic few wish to discuss openly. The euphemism "Slim" refers to the Grim Reaper, the spectre of death in the form of an emaciated being who brings on the dreaded HIV/AIDS.

This is the conversation between a father and his eldest son who faces the grim spectre of HIV/AIDS. The young man bravely fights to survive. He denies that "Slim" is about to take his life. He sits under the shade of a Mpundu tree, awaiting his fate. Banished from his ancestral home, he will face death alone. The elder is first to speak:

"You are no longer my child
No longer my trustworthy child
Once mine, you will soon be replaced by another
Ah! I see I have shocked you
Sit down and tell me all the news you have for me"

Under the shade of Mpundu tree
Tears streaming down to the souls of his feet

Taken aback, and barely able to open
his lips, the son replies,

"You have no idea how much I have been sweating
at night!
With these persistent diarrheas, how will I sit down?
With this chronic weakness, who will serve me?
With this documented fever, who will cool me down?
With this irregular heartbeat, who will come to my aid?
With ugly scabies, who will squeeze my oozing pus?
With these skeleton legs that can't put me in motion
Who will fetch me my crutches?
My family and community will now throw me out."

Under the shade of Mpundu tree
Tears streaming down to the soles of his feet

"Everybody is scared of you
No one wants to be associated with you
Not your mother, father, brothers, sisters and
the community
Except perhaps your wife and children and grandparents
Your big sunken eyes, sharp pointed countable ribs
Diarrhea like water running from a tap,
You have harvested all the green leaves
Boils and herpes have taken their strategic positions

Your dignity is gone, you are nothing
Look at your hair, sparsely populated,
Curled like that of a new born baby
They will throw you food as to a dog"

Under the shade of Mpundu tree
Tears streaming down to the soles of his feet

"I am not afraid of Slim
You are mistaken – I do belong to you
You want to taint my family black
Slim attacks the poor, uneducated, and lazy in rural places
He is not for beautiful and handsome people like me and
my family
He is an ugly chameleon with white big cotton eyes,
I am not his child, I am busy at university studying
Ask my mother and father how it can be me
A bad seed in my own family! No never!
You are out of your mind"

Under the shade of Mpundu tree
Tears streaming down to the soles of his feet

"Have you not seen, are you so blind?
Raindrops roll down the cheeks of your wife and children
Isolated to a narrow dark house of banana leaves
You are far out from your parents' home
No one wants to touch you, no one
to give even a drop of water

No one wants to sit next or share clothes with you
Appetite is gone, sleep is futile
Your stomach is full of butterflies
Sharp pain penetrates deep down, every nerve alive
You call for euthanasia for not even
ARVs can ease the pain"

Waiting, waiting, you wait for the clock to stop
A casket waits for you to join Slim's choir

by Patricia Nyanchama Makori
10/2015

Mzungu says: The Mpundu Tree is associated with David Livingstone, the famous Scottish missionary and explorer who died at Ilala near Victoria Falls. Livingstone's heart had been buried under a mpundu tree. Common to central and east Africa, its fruits are bitter to the taste. Dr Livingstone was buried in Westminster Abbey, his heart left in his beloved Africa.

Mum — why did you give me your back?

(An Orphan Child's Lament)

From the top of the ladder
To the bottom of the ladder
From high table
Down to no table
From high voltage degree of richness
To sinking deep down to a church mouse
From high class Cadillac vehicles
To not even a wheelbarrow
From eating in a five star hotel
To fighting for food from the dustbin with dogs and rats
From life in the beautiful city
To a quiet ugly rural environment
From a well-lit and fenced electric house
To a polythene lit unprotected house
From sleeping in a four by six bed
To sleeping on a goat skin

Mum is it because you gave me your back?

From national school to a rural day school
Dropping out of school, graduating to the streets,
Dropping out of school to selling drugs
Dropping out of school to stealing and killing
Dropping out of school to law breaking
Dropping out of school to early marriage
Dropping out of school sinking into a pit
Dropping out of school to committing suicide
Dropping from school to jail

I am calling you mum to come to my rescue
Mum since the cruel hand of death snatched you from us
We are unaccepted in our father's land
You have been blamed as the cause of our father's death
We have been labeled as a bad omen to the family
Even when you are rotting in your grave
I can recall when dad begged you for forgiveness
Forgiveness for infecting you with HIV/AIDs.
He sent a letter to his family passing the same information
But it fell into deaf ears
Now am dressed in tattered clothes
No shoes any more, no sanitary pads
Jiggers have infested my toes;
I have no pin to pull them out
Lice and bedbugs celebrate on my blood
They suck my flesh day and night
I am a dying well with only brackish water left
When strolling on the streets
My breasts sway from East to West, North to South
I cannot afford a second hand brassiere
My only pants wash and wear are full of holes
Potholes that are beyond the tailor's repair

Mum can you hear me
I thought you would always be there for me
I have no one to turn to
Why are you cold, quiet
I can recall how you used to smile
I can recall your last cry of pain
You promised not to leave me alone when you are gone

Like an orphan in an orphanage
I have my nest on the streets
I spread my rags as a mattress
Cover myself with polythene as a blanket
At dawn I rise up, with all sorts of garbage
Head for a long endless journey
I am tired of being harassed
Mum if you want to communicate to me
Please ask my father to come to my rescue
I am ready to go — I am going

by Patricia Nyanchama Makori
08/2015

Orphan Kids of Kakamega

The main road north from Kisumu leads to Kakamega
heartland of the Luhya people.
hot winds blow in from the west,
up the valley from Lake Victoria
carrying rain over the Nandi Escarpment.

Kenya's rainforest, feast for the senses,
unique, vibrant, teeming with the life of
hundreds of butterfly species
grey parrots, blue turacos, hornbills
forest raptors, snakes, primates.
home to Mama Mutter
ancient tree of medicinal cure
rooted in Kakamega Forest.

Mt. Elgon to the north,
and Kirinyaga's Mt. Kenya
hide their faces at a land
ravaged by poverty and disease.

Weeping stone of Ilesi sighs
during spring a constant stream of tears
flow down its time worn sides.

Motherless children
the neglected and lonely,
broken hearts with muted voices,
too young to face the blackness
of HIV/AIDS.

Listen to their silence

'Orphan Kids of Kakamega'.

Under the Acacia Tree Anthology
06/2004

CHAPTER 7:

Abandoned Treasures

"The eye never forgets what the heart has seen"

Kenyan proverb

Mzungu says: Since 2012 CES has partnered with Divine Providence Orphanage in Kakamega. Currently there are 200 children ages day-old to 18 years living there. CES provides mosquito nets, food, clothing, toys, agri-consulting and friendship activities through the CES Alumni. This chapter is dedicated to those children who receive care and support through the Benedictine Sisters of Divine Providence. Children are orphaned and abandoned for many reasons but principally as a result of the HIV/AIDS pandemic in Kenya.

Nobody's Child

Look for me in the slums of Mathare
find me sleeping in the gutters of Eastleigh
begging for a shilling on the streets of Nairobi
Nobody's child

Pain that touches me oh so deep
eyes so dry I cannot weep
walking a path that's far too steep
Nobody's child

None to give me food or shelter
gone the touch of a loving mother
alone, the brutal fact of the matter
Nobody's child

Voiceless I cry out – no one is listening
invisible I walk about – none are caring
darkness surrounds – though sun is shining on
Nobody's child

Hoping to find what I'm craving, seeking
freedom and hope and a future believing
that one day a new name I'll be receiving
Somebody's child

Raising the banner of hope for tomorrow
I'm ready to work hard on lessons to follow
if given the chance then you'll be my hero
Your loving child

Under the Acacia Tree Anthology
07/2009

Not Enough

Sweet morning dew graces empty fields
of maize and sugar cane recently harvested;
not enough food to feed the hungry.

Hot sun rises over red-brown mud huts,
cracks breaking in a thousand directions;
not enough shelter to deflect the burning ray.

Women labouring, gathering, working,
men waiting for something to happen;
not enough justice to cover the loss.

Orphan children carrying infants too young
to feel the pain except in their belly;
not enough strength to carry on.

Parent-child is forced into labour
never parented, never embraced;
not enough love to go 'round.

Relentless human tragedy races
like a tsunami out of control;
not enough will to turn the tide.

Why?

When there is more than enough
to keep the dogs of HIV/AIDS at bay.

Under the Acacia Tree Anthology
05/2008

Mzungu says: Here's an amazing story about a recent CES graduate from Namundera SS giving his school uniform to a new student who could not afford one. Without a uniform to wear, students cannot attend school. Now that's tragic. CES ensures all students on secondary scholarship have two sets of clothes to wear for school purposes.

A DAY THAT CHANGED MY LIFE

Elicah Wandera, Form 4 Namundera SS

The demise of our father on 12th November 2002 left the five of us to live from hand to mouth. It was now two years later, and I was struggling with education in Standard Four. I never thought I would finish my primary education. I knew it was the key to life but I seemed to be losing mine to fate. I needed someone to help me through this psychological torture. I longed for the day – the day I am writing about.

Getting the basic needs were rare in our family – like lunar eclipses. I was frequently absent from school. I could only attend the next day if we had our meagre supper the previous evening. This greatly affected my performance in class. My uniform used to be a long wing-like shirt that my dad had bought me. It made me look like a girl. My friends laughed. They always called me names. I wondered what kind of life I was living. I regretted my dad dying, leaving us so young. We still needed his guidance. I wished he were peeping through the clouds to see the problems we were encountering. I longed for the day – the day I am writing about.

Their laughter almost made me give up my education. The free primary education introduced by President Mwai Kibaki in 2003 gave me impetus to work hard. But I still needed more assistance. Relatives had given up on our family. I could not ask them for support. We had no food and I was sliding into a state of hopelessness. The little hope I had kept telling me if I would sit for the national examination with my classmates then I would find a key to the padlock of my heart's door. I clung to my prayers waiting for the day – the day I am writing about.

Results were now about to come out. I could not sleep since I wondered what kind of laughter I would get from relatives if I failed the exams. After the release of results they were left in a fix. The flying colours I had passed with made my mother go bananas with happiness. She wondered and doubted whether I had sat for the exams myself or had cheated.

Passing the exams was like opening a Pandora's box. The news spread wide across the village like fires in the African wilderness. People commented, "Where will he go with all those marks? He wasted his money for registration and his energy by going to school regularly." This is when I cursed the day I was born.

My mother tried to engage in the business of selling fish to pay for my school fees. That was not enough. I knew I was now in hot soup. I decided to go look after our cousin's cows to get the money to secure admission at any school. I wondered if my life would ever change. I kept on praying to God waiting for the day – the day I am writing about.

February 1st, I went to pick up a letter of admission from my former primary school. The fee structure at Butonge High School was too high. I feared presenting it to my mother. She looked at it tearfully. I saw my hope disintegrate as two big tear drops fell on the earthen floor in our smoky kitchen.

Two weeks passed. Realizing all my friends were in school, I went to one of the local day schools in our area. I met students in pink uniforms. They were mixing chemicals in some thin glasses outside in the field. I went straight and stood next to them. I realized it was a Form 1 Chemistry lesson. I cried and went home hoping for the day – the day I am writing about.

Dressed in my primary school uniform I decided the next day to take my two exercise books and go to the same school. I met students on parade. When the teacher on duty asked for any student to pray, I decided to do the prayers. When students dispersed to class, I was left at the parade ground like a lost chicken. A teacher told me to go home. A soft sob turned into uncontrollable spasms. I left sorrowing.

That evening a student from the same school came and told me that I was required at school. He did not say why. I packed my books, ironed my primary school shirt with an iron box filled with charcoal. Next morning I attended school. I was called by the Guiding and Counselling teacher who asked questions. I answered as tears cascaded down my potato cheeks. I was taken into another office and given an admission letter. My heart smiled. That same day I received a second hand uniform from James Wasike a former student, now a CES graduate.

I was admitted and told that I would be considered for a CES scholarship. All I had to do was emerge position one in the class at the end of term exam. If I told you I was not happy I would be lying. I knew I would make it. By the end of the term I had kept my promise. I was number one in the class. I was given a CES form to fill out. This was the day – the day I am writing about. I was transformed.

Standing on the shoulders of CES, I can now see where I am heading: the vision of my eyes is the vision of my heart. As I celebrate this day, join me in singing the following poem:

Cry of An Orphan

Death you are bad
you fetched my father
left me alone — a bird, sad
with only my mother.
if you were a firewood
I would have fixed you with fire.

You make my neighbour
like a rogue robber
to wholly hate me.
you make my mother
to be silently stressed.
if you were a stone
I would smash you into the sea.

I do not feel good
because of missing food,
you make me a fool
because of missing school.
if you were my skin
I would have jumped out of you.

But CES, our only organization
you made me
you stand with me
though I am an orphan it is true
I can!
if education is a padlock
you be my clear key.

Elicah Wandera, Namundera SS

Part III

Dream No Small Dreams

CHAPTER 8:

From Tragedy to Hope

"Life is short, so leave a legacy"

Kenyan proverb

Mzungu says: I visited the Kakamega area in September 2018, and with the help of people including Malik Khaemba (who did most of the driving), Sarah Nabongo and Melvin Wafula, I interviewed about thirty people who have been impacted by CES. Four of those interviews are transcribed below. But first a little background.

The dream of building a secondary school at Musaga began in 2008. A small group of twenty boys were meeting with a teacher under a tree to learn. Without any classroom or school facilities the quality of learning was limited. They had nowhere to turn. The villagers could not contribute and the Board of Managers saw students slowly leave for other schools. They needed a local school because the next alternative for some was a twenty kilometre walk each day.

CES Kenya Chairman Ben Udoto loves to tell the story of how he grew up in Musaga village back in the early 1950's. He first learned to read and write in the sand under the shade of a mango tree. There were no classrooms, no desks and nothing to write on. There was however the most important item, a dedicated teacher. Ben was a willing learner who used his index finger to carve out numbers and letters on the ground. He went on to obtain an MEd in Administration and had a successful career as an educator and Principal at Kaimosi Teachers College. So when the plea to build a school was considered by CES, Ben 'Mr Chairman' Udoto had a particular interest in what was to become the most ambitious building project CES has undertaken.

The school was built, one classroom at a time and in 2011 the first group of students in Form 1 began their education at Musaga SS. By 2014 all four grades were in place and in 2016 a kitchen was added to the school. Musaga SS now has 480 girls and boys and it is a thriving education community.

Musaga School was built out of story of loss and tragedy. Deanna O'Neill was part of the Thunder Bay chapter of CES Canada. She supported CES and it was her dream to one day visit Kenya. Sadly, after a brief battle with cancer, she died before that could happen. There was a huge outpouring of love and support for Deanna's family. Fundraisers, bake sales, athletic events and marathon runs raised significant funds for the school.

Others in Kenya took on special projects like the connection to bring electricity to the school. Local carpenters built desks and chairs for the students who now began to return to Musaga SS. Slowly, little by little, progress was made.

This is an inspiring story that shows how out of tragedy, good things can emerge. In Deanna's honour and in support of a charity she loved, Musaga SS was dedicated on July 3, 2013. There is a beautiful bronze coloured sign in front of the Admin block that commemorates the official opening. Lynn Zolinsky, Deanna's mother dedicated the school before an assembled group of over 1000 people. Thanks and huge appreciation go to the family and friends of Deanna O'Neill in Thunder Bay, Ontario who have made this possible.

Sheila Nasindu is a CES graduate (2010) of Musaga SS. She is celebrated for her powerful dramatic presentations. 'We Are Because You Were' is a beautiful piece honouring Deanna O'Neil.

We Are Because You Were

Musaga SS, haven for the needy, with you I join
those who honour the life of Deanna O'Neil.

Out of grief I rise to curse the winds of death
whose purpose was concealed from
doctors, interceders, advocates of life.

As I pray, I mourn the demise of the heroine soul.
In pain and in vain I search for answers,
sadly I find none.

Death does not bow to hospitals or
wait on churches that challenge its mandate.
The innocent are taken all too soon.

As we celebrate the new Musaga,
we cherish the wonderful people of CES
and think of Deanna, loving daughter of Lynn Zolinski,
thankful for her sacrifice to the needy.

Overwhelmed by a spirit of optimism,
I now turn to God in thanks.
Deanna's departure is not in vain,
Her memory is raised to the heights
as she has been been promoted to glory.
We are because you were.

Musaga SS (09/2018)

Nashon UDOTO
Chairman, Friends School Musaga

Starting a school was a community idea. My brother worked with CES, so when he introduced the community project to CES, they came and started building the school right from scratch. There was no building here previously. They started building the tuition block, they put up the modern kitchen, they have helped us put up a temporary dining hall for the students. Now we have eight classrooms. And the students who benefit from this are very happy.

Our students come from very poor and humble backgrounds. Without CES, most of them could have dropped out after primary school. CES sponsors students who are economically poor, hard working and disciplined. So when CES provides tuition fees, they know there is a future for them. Some of them have really excelled and have gone on to college. Those who do very well in the national exam apply to CES to help sponsor them through college. We have several students who have gone to university. We hope when they come back they provide services to the school and the community.

Many of our students' parents are poor, they can't afford fees. These homes have not just two or three children, sometimes they have more than five. But they can only pay fees for one or two. Those who can't afford to go to secondary school end up doing casual labour for people. Others end up just drinking, and maybe become criminals on the way and they start doing all manner of unlawful things – we feel very bad.

Mzungu asks, "I've heard that in some cultures, parents tend to show
preference for educating their boy children rather than their girls
– is that the case here?"

No, it is not like that here. There is equal opportunity and the government is now coming in and saying they will provide free tuition for all kids who cannot afford to go to secondary school. Many of them are being sponsored by the government; however, it is not enough. Students only have to pay for basics like lunch, books and a school uniform. It's not that schools like sending them home. You send them home, they come back with the parent and a story, but not with money. Everyone is trying. Some plant sugar cane, some make bricks and others volunteer so their child can attend school. When there is no money, parents give what they can.

Joseph WANDERA
Founding Principal, Musaga SS

I was posted to this school as Principal. My home is nearby. I got a letter from a school called Musaga Secondary to start and open as its first principal. When I came around, there was nothing. I was met by the PTA Chairman, who said that they would be building here on this piece of land. I said, "Where are the students?" He replied, "At the church down there."

I walked to the nearby Baptist church where I found some students sitting on benches. Others were sitting under a tree. There were no classrooms, no office buildings, nothing. So I just accepted. I told him that since there are students around, we shall just start off from where they are.

In 2010, CES President Michael Frederiksen came around. When he showed such an interest in our situation, I was very happy. He came with some colleagues from Canada and we began to build. In 2013 there was a group of over 20 white people from a place called Thunder Bay. We had a big celebration with music and dancing as we officially dedicated the new school.

Mr. Malik Khaemba told me about CES, Community Education Services. We agreed to begin funding twelve students. They were both bright and needy. When you look at their homes they are actually wanting, because their parents are very poor. But when you look at the child, the child is bright with a lot of potential.

One of those students was from a neighbouring home. The father is a watchman here at the school. He didn't have money to pay school fees. His daughter was bright and now she is at the university. I'm really proud of that girl. Sheila Nasindu started from Musaga SS, Form One up to Form Four, and she made it. She's among the pioneers of my school here.

CES first started funding poor students and later began to construct classrooms and other facilities. If it were not for CES, I'm sure that this school would be just two or three classrooms. The money to build was a gift from CES. The parents could not support the building project as they are not well off. They just pay fees of about 10,000 Kenyan Shillings (CDN$130), and that's a problem. There is never enough to go around.

CES put up eight classrooms, plus a kitchen. There is a temporary dining hall, because the students need a place where they can eat their food. With the CES funding, I made sure that the money was used for bricks, cement, mortar, roofing and trusses. I recall that Michael came several times from Canada and confirmed that the work was done. in 2016 we opened the new kitchen. I always remember Michael insisting that we keep the old mud and thatch roof kitchen, and use it for some cooking and storage of food. That way, students would know and appreciate Musaga's humble beginnings and how far the school community had progressed.

The school here has a catchment area. If a school doesn't perform, the parents tend to take their children to a school where they feel they will get a good education. This means that the students remaining at the school are not good material. When a high school performs well, it is because students from the primary schools have achieved at least 350/500 marks in the KCPE. And also when a school is well-staffed, and properly managed, the parents have no problem sending their children to that school. So, simply providing a good education is what we do. And parents have responded by sending their children to us.

A young school compared to the others around, this one is ahead of many. Recently, I came back after retirement and found that many of the students have performed well and some have gone to the university. When I first came here, there were board members who thought that Musaga SS would not reach this level that soon. Now some pupils are fighting to come here. I am so proud of my school community and grateful to CES for all they have done to make this a great school.

Dorcas WAFULA
Teacher, Friends School Musaga
CES Liaison Staff Member and Counsellor

CES is a wonderful organization that has come to serve the needs of needy students in the community. These now can at least be like the others, able to learn and move ahead. We are very grateful to the CES community. Recently we attended a conference with the candidates that are going to sit for their Form Four exam. The CES Alumni group were also there to teach and mentor students from all the CES schools. They were excellent role models and our students were encouraged to emulate them and strive to study at the university level.

CES is a great practical help to us in that they also provide for the students' basic needs. That includes sanitary towels for the girls. There is also soap, hand cream, shoe polish, shoe brushes, toothbrushes so that a student can be comfortable in coming to school.

The help from CES means that they are in school full time. Students don't need to take time to go home for the fee balance. Since students get enough time to study, and they will have no excuse about failing exams.

We know that some girls don't have necessities like sanitary towels. Menstruation is a natural thing, part of life. Sometimes periods come by accident, without warning. To help with this, I talked to the deputy, and she went and purchased a full box of supplies. When a girl is in need, she makes a request and I give her a pad. This way, we reduce the distraction of going in and out of the classroom, especially when it's near the end of the month cycle. When a students says, "Madam, I'm not feeling well", we ask about the situation and sometimes provide a painkiller and that is enough. Some students would rather tell a friend or a classmate to go and tell Madam, and then the girl comes to Madam saying, "so-and-so is in trouble." We know what is happening and do everything possible to assist our girls.

For me, CES is like a family. When you look into the students' backgrounds, you'll find that maybe their parents are divorced or deceased. So when Michael comes for a visit, they consider him as a father. They get that fatherly love. We also have gatherings where students attend conferences and events like the Canada Day Run. They travel and meet other CES students to interact, and socialize. It's more like a family. It brings them together, it gives them joy. It's just that sometimes maybe they are not open to you people (Canadians), but when we just sit back with them and make jokes, it's like a family. It gives them peace, which they don't get back at home.

Billington ASIENWA
Principal, Friends School Musaga

I came here in mid last year (2018), and from day one I was able to feel the impact of CES. All the classrooms we have, apart from two science blocks, are courtesy of CES.

There are also some students who are being sponsored by CES, and it is not just Form One up to Form Four; they even go beyond to support those who are going to various universities. Students are interviewed and there are some who are given a full scholarship, and others a partial scholarship.

To us we feel that sponsoring a student is a great motivation to a learner who has a dream. It's even more important if they have a challenge paying school fees. Students will say, "Somebody I don't know has empathized with me and is paying for my schooling; the only way I can pay that back is to work hard and pass. Then the donors will feel their money didn't go to waste."

That is what is generally expected of a student who is being assisted. But you know that a coin has two sides. There are also some who are selected, but they don't actually internalize or think about how somebody has sacrificed in order for them to pursue their education. Such students don't have a dream. They don't even feel it is a privilege for somebody to give them a chance to go through school. It may be due to their home environment – there are very few role models who can be used as examples for students to work hard. They look at their parents who have not gone to school and do not value education as necessary. So even when given a chance to be helped they don't really take advantage because they think, "Look at my parents, they never went to school and here they are. I can be the same."

There are situations where we send them home to bring school fees, and then you find a parent who will tell them, "I never went to school, so you might as well stay home." These messages impact negatively on the children, and it affects their performance.

Particularly in this geographic rural area, we still have a very big problem with education. Many parents have not embraced the importance of education. They feel it is just a process that at one time in life a child ought to be in school, irrespective of what they learn. Children who come from such homes don't work hard when they are in school, whether you help them or not.

Students are assigned homework, but when they get home most of them don't have electricity. They rely on kerosene lanterns, but no fuel is available. When they come back the next day their assignments have not been done. Some get so demoralized because their parents are not helping them.

When we have meetings with the parents, we normally agree that there are three people involved – the parent, the student and the teacher. To succeed we must work as a team. When one does not take up his or her role well, we definitely cannot succeed.

It has taken time for many parents in this area to realize the importance of education. In this place, it looks almost normal for a student to drop out of school. This has led to some having early marriages. We have a very recent example where one of our girls who qualified to go to the university last year, just decided to get married. We had to struggle with the provincial administration to have this girl come back to pursue her education. There are so many students who wanted the opportunity she had. Yet, here is one who has made it, but does not look at the value of that certificate.

As a community we still have a long way to go. It's now impacting on our students that education is the only key that leads to success. Why am I saying this? There are some students who have been sponsored by CES, and they have gone through to the universities. They are now working and parents are so proud of them because now they're taking care of their poor homes. Now we sometimes invite former students, CES graduates to come to our school and talk to our students. They are good examples, mentors and they inspire the younger ones to work hard and create a better life.

Now I'm trying to imagine what Musaga SS would be if CES had not built all these classrooms. I just don't know whether the school would even exist. The parents had their own building project they were unable to complete, including an unroofed building. CES has done a great thing for our community.

That unfinished building is a very good example we can use with our parents who refused to cooperate. We shall tell them that somebody (CES) came in and assisted us – and now look, these are the type of students we are getting. This changes their perception towards building and developing their own schools. It's actually a lifetime lesson that we have to keep giving them, and it's also about exposure to new ideas.

That is why as a school we're trying to expose them to new ideas in two ways. One is to take them outside the school so that they can also learn what is happening outside. Two, we bring in speakers, people who are seasoned in various fields to talk to them. That way, the students can know, if they want to pursue this type of career, these are the subjects required – and above all they should work hard.

We normally tell them it is very difficult to be a failure in life, but it is very easy to be successful. It all just depends on what you just decide. We support a positive attitude that says, "Yes, it is possible, I can do it no matter how slow it will be, but I will be able to do it." It will take time, but we are very grateful because we are able to see some fruits that are coming out of the whole program. If we had more sponsorship it would attract more students and therefore the output would also be favourable. But we cannot cry, because half a loaf is better than none.

We also have a bicycle program through World Vision, where students who come from far are given bicycles. The intention being, you arrive in school early so that you can attend to your lessons. All of these programs are actually helping us to move faster. Otherwise, without this type of support maybe it could have taken too long to reach where we have reached.

We also teach the students about volunteering and giving back. It's not just a matter of thinking, "I was helped and now I'm successful." It is very important to look back so that you also give back to society, so that you can also touch another soul somewhere, one that is innocent and unable to move ahead. That way, God can also bless you. You succeeded because somebody sacrificed. The best way to appreciate that is when you turn back and also lift up somebody who is down.

We have seen that the CES alumni group is doing a lot of good for these students. That's because they visit schools to talk to the students. They tell the students that they should not stop chasing their dream. That dream is very important. Think about what it will take to get you where you want to go in life. After all, we have so many people who have come from very humble beginnings and they never got discouraged, they still made it in life.

Carl Friesen (left) interviews Joseph Wandera, retired first Principal of Musaga Secondary School. Here, Mr. Wandera explains the history and growth of the school, now with over 480 students enrolled.

A group of girls walking together on their way to Musaga Secondary School – cheerful and eager to learn. CES built this school with funding from Canadian donors. Officially opened in 2013, it was dedicated in memory of CES volunteer Deanna O'Neal, Thunder Bay Ontario.

The CES PAD Project supports girls, providing them with education and feminine hygiene resources. This builds their self-esteem and ensures stronger attendance in school without interruption in learning. Here, retired Canadian nurse Marie McKay teaches and encourages our CES girls. Marie served in western Kenya for 20 years and was instrumental in guiding CES, particularly in its early years.

CES Alumna Doris Miroya (left) tutors Form 4 Musaga SS students who are preparing for their KCSE (Kenya Certificate of Secondary Education) exams.

Students at Ibinzo Girls Secondary School receive their daily portion of ugali (porridge made with ground corn flour), lentils and beans. Rice and chicken is served on special occasions. CES provides a hot meal and tea each day to sponsored students.

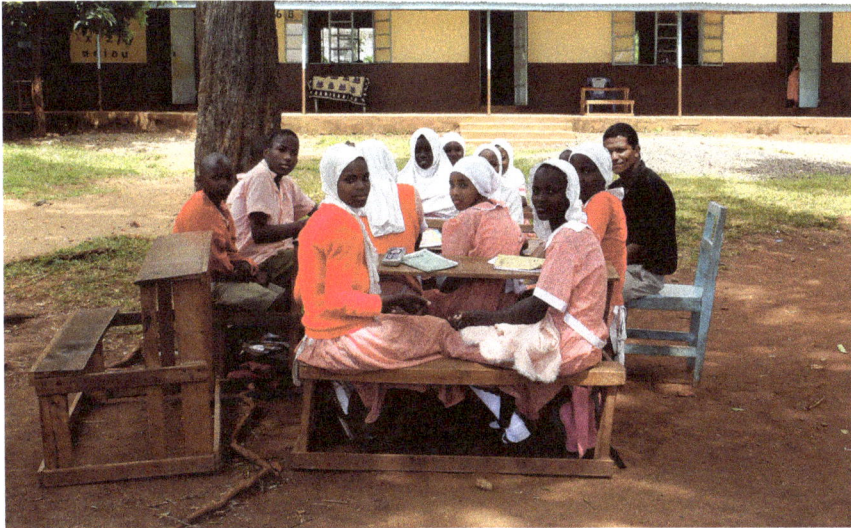

Students at Kakamega Muslim Secondary School are taught Religious Instruction, usually in an outdoor setting. Student demographics at KMSS are 80 percent Muslim and 20 percent Christian. They are free to choose the Ministry of Education curriculum that reflects their own faith.

One of the biggest problems facing Kenyan education is access to clean water for hygiene and drinking. In many schools students bring their own water supplies, often scooped from a contaminated water source. Here a student fills her drinking cup from a well funded by the Church of the Redeemer community — Rosseau, Ontario.

CHAPTER 9:

Challenges and Opportunities

"The road to success is always under construction"

Kenyan proverb

by Hesborne Omolo Otieno
Principal, Kakamega Muslim Secondary School

To be honest CES has impacted very positively for me as a principal. This school targets students from the very low in our society, that is the very poor. So, naturally they have challenges with fee payments, challenges with finding social and educational support. When CES comes on board, it takes care of their fees and by extension, even some of the meals that cannot be provided in school. The student's mind-set is relaxed and for that reason they are able to focus and do better academically.

For other schools I can't say, but in my school CES has really supported the very needy. As teachers, we try to reach out to those who are desperate. Also, when academically they have shown promise we give them help, and a good number of them have found their way even up to the university.

CES tells us the number they wish to fund. Finding the right students and vetting them takes place within the school. Then we give CES the names. One factor we look for is their level of academic achievement. Two, we look at the family background, because we really want those who are very poor and needy, especially those that are orphaned.

Each term the CES team led by Mr. Malik comes and talks to the students. They also check their report cards and provide a mentorship program. It is important that CES knows there is value for the money they are paying. Then they make a follow up with individual respective schools and students. When they arrive here at Kakamega Muslim SS, I call the students and the CES team members sit here with them and they talk about their report card. They also challenge them to do their best, and they also find out the challenges and what they may be going through.

I have told our students, "You know, for people to support you or sponsor you, they really sacrifice. So even you as a person, you also need to make some little sacrifice on your part. And part of the sacrifice you can make is to improve your character and add value to your life academically and as a person."

We are trying to move from their story, which was dark and often bad, to give them some light offered through CES. And this means that the whole person, the totality and the holistic nature of the human being is transformed.

You see, like now CES Kenya is even going forward. They support students past the secondary level. When students join university, CES still follows them up to that level just to ensure that continuity is there. This is very good. Because, if you take the project and leave it halfway; meaning, a student goes through Form Four and you stop there, you have just given the child some little light. But now CES follows graduates graduates even up to university. And they are also supported by the alumni group. I feel that is the right way to go.

CES Kenya has really impacted this community whereby it has improved socially and economically. For the vulnerable students who were unable to go to school, CES has taken over the load of paying school fees.

This community has really been challenged. We have some students, whose parents perished, so they don't have a mother or a father. They are total orphans. When you look at the family they come from, it is so horrible. And these students, when they come to school, they show a sign of being bright in school. Their lives now have some hope.

CES has done a wonderful job in this community. We have here parents, who died because of HIV/AIDS. And maybe some of these students were born HIV positive. And in this community, you'll find such students being side-lined. And when that happens, they despair in life. CES has really played a big role whereby they come in and talk to these students. They talk to them openly and students begin to share their position health wise. They are encouraged that this is not the end of their life. They buy that and now most of them have really gone far.

Secondly, if I can add to that, Africans have long believed in a kind of socialism. You stay together in one homestead. Imagine a situation in which my nephew's father and mother have gone, and he knows that I am an uncle. Sometimes, it could be that with these kids, the only adult person they know is me. The fact is I am also overwhelmed by my own children. They could all be in that same age bracket. And then these additional ones are added to my responsibilities. The person now taking care of these children may be a grandfather or a grandmother, very old. And they have stopped working. Then now you have grandchildren, all looking to you for support. This is where CES comes in to take some of that burden from these elderly people.

When a student is sent away to collect school fees from their home, the problem may be that the family is totally poor. Heads of the families are often very old, have never gone to school, and don't know the value of education. CES really helps to improve the economical part of that family. CES takes this student to a higher level and helps to secure a better place in life, thus improving the family lifestyle.

Because of this background support, we as parents of this community have really appreciated the work of CES Kenya. The contract on fee payment is between the parent and the school, not the learner. But in many cases the parents are not even there. And this is now the point where CES is coming in. So when you support a child, it's like you are taking the responsibility. When the child needs fees, he or she goes to the CES office. CES then becomes like the parent to these needy children.

In Kenya we have some support programs where the county and national governments give sponsorships. Many elderly people who are guardians for many, may be illiterate, unable to fill those registration forms. I had a boy who was forced to work for people in the village to earn a living. If you gave him twenty or thirty shillings, that is what he was using to survive on, pay his rent and also pay his school fees. So it becomes a very sad situation and very frustrating.

In the setup where I am in, it is a Muslim sponsored school. Muslims really value the idea of socialism. One sponsor or guardian could have ten children in school. These are not all his biological children and it causes much stress to support everyone in their education. Sometimes, a student had to stay home for several years because no one could support school fees. Then a good Samaritan somewhere in the village notices that this child still has the ability and is willing to go to school. They attend school, the first semester fees is paid for and then that person disappears. So you have a young student with no parent – what do you? Even if you send them away – where to? Often we are just forced to let them go through the system, they survive at the expense of others, which is very difficult. The alternative is the student drops out of school.

The government has expanded its support for education. Right now, the parents are just responsible for their children's upkeep. The government is taking the bulk of the fees, so that is kind of reducing the pressure on the parents. However, that support is not regular and dependable. Life is going on, the expenses are going on, you need to pay workers, you need to buy the teaching materials and the money is not there.

Once students have graduated, the government accepts them to join vocational technical schools. I have two students who came to me, former CES sponsored students. They had secured a chance to study at Sigalagala Technical College. They were supposed to join in September, but the first down payment promised by the government did not arrive. The students are still at home. They feel very inferior and the situation is now desperate. CES Kenya has promised a partial scholarship so there is still hope. So there are so many challenges facing these vulnerable students.

Mzungu says: The challenges are great…so too are the rewards. But with nowhere and no one to turn to, it is not easy to create a spirit of hope for those who feel that life has passed them by. Here's a question with a compelling emotional component.

Why Me?

Why me?
sent home yet again, twice this term
humiliated I slink out the back gate
with no place to go
none to turn to … o yes,
my aged auntie in Mumias
maybe she will take me in for one night

Why me?
how can I return to school
without my school fees paid in full
embarrassed, angry and sad all at once
through my tears I see I am not the only one
walking this dirt road
I recognize the blue, pink, green uniforms
from other schools — the same story
we're in this together

Why me?
five hour walk over hot tarmac
thrice pushed into the ditch by an overloaded truck
carrying useless tires with no tread
to be sold for new shoes I cannot afford
hungry I chew on some sugar
yet the pain does not subside
and even if my aunt could spare a few shillings
these would not come close
to the 5000 shillings needed to return.

Why me?
an offer to pay for my fees is tempting
yet it comes with a stipulation and a risk
that may take my life forever
down a path of sickness to death.

Why me?
all I want is a chance to learn
without fear of hearing her calling out my name
"you cannot return until you have your school fees."
the words bite hard at my soul
I cannot bear it – my dream is slipping
it happened last term in Form 1
that was the last time I spoke to my mother
Aids took her life as it had my father's the year before
I would rather go on a hunger vigil for fourteen days
I have done so before and at least I can bear that pain

Why me?
if I cannot pay my school fee
will I ever see the inside of a classroom again?
can I complete another prep or write the KCSE
or will my life be an unending cycle
searching for firewood, finding water
living from hand to mouth for the rest of my days?

Why me?
what have I done to deserve such a fate
when all around me others eat maize and beans
and go to school with shoes on their feet.
I must have done something wrong

by Patricia Nyanchama Makori
10/2016

CHAPTER 10:

Heart of Service

"A Good Name Shines in the Dark"

Kenyan proverb

Mzungu says: The following three stories take place at different times. Each reflects the joy of service as experienced by CES volunteers from Canada.

MY TIME WITH SHARYN

From a blog post by CES Canada board member Tom Conant, written in 2013

I was lying back on the wooden bench in the inner courtyard of the Kenyan Natural Museum, basking in the sun of a warm February day. A cool breeze blew through the trees above me, creating a natural pleasant sound behind the chirping of the birds. I could hear a traditional Kenyan band playing somewhere nearby, undoubtedly for the *mzungu* tourists arriving each day.

After being in the country for six months, my time was almost up and I was due to fly back to Canada in just a few days. After the hustle and bustle, the controlled mayhem that seemed to be the theme of the previous months, this moment in time was one of peaceful bliss. Despite being right near the heart of the busy city of Nairobi, this particular spot seemed be located in a vacuum of noise.

Sharyn Poole called me and begged for forgiveness. As she explained, she was caught in the middle of the infamous midday Nairobi traffic and that she would be late. I assured her this was no problem, not just because I wanted to savour the serenity for as long as possible, but also because my only plan for the day was to spend it with Sharyn at the museum. "When she gets here she gets here", I thought.

I was lucky to have her as a companion for the day's event. While I was happy to have a few days to myself with no work or schools to visit, I am not one to spend too much time alone. Sharyn, who happened to be in the city, enthusiastically agreed to join me at the museum. That was Sharyn, as I had come to know her. She was never one to say 'No' to an offer unless there was a good reason to refuse.

The phone rang beside me and I knew she had arrived and was looking for me. Initially, however, she was hard to find. It is quite easy to spot a *mzungu* in a Nairobi crowd, but on this occasion she was nowhere to be found. I searched the front entrance, the reception hall, even back to where I had been laying in the courtyard, to no avail. This elder *mzungu* seemed to have vanished right into the woodwork. It was then that the thought occurred to me, and I had a feeling that I should follow the rhythm.

And there she was. I walked down the pathway and arrived at the museum amphitheatre to find this vivacious woman standing beside the musicians who were beating away at their traditional Kenyan instruments. Her love for music and her fearless attitude had allowed her to walk right up to the band members, despite her being the only person in the audience at that moment.

As always, she was dressed in a most aesthetically appealing combination of jewellery and clothing, with a style undoubtedly of her own arrangement. She noticed me standing at the top of the open air theatre, staring at her below, and she waved for me to join her. Always a lover of the spontaneous and impromptu, I could see that we would be spending some time with these musicians, soaking in the sounds. To this I was more than happy to comply. I made my way down the eight levels of seating and we greeted each other fondly, like old friends reuniting after years being part.

For the next hour we sat side by side, tapping in unison as the music swept over us. As I write this I am re-listening to the recordings I had made of that performance; and from these, I remind myself why it is I got along so well with Mrs. Sharyn. She was the kind of person that had a deep passion for 'the other', meaning that which is not of the usual but more the unfamiliar. Sharyn and I both shared a deep desire to saturate ourselves in what is novel, and the day's performance was exactly that.

I am currently listening to over an hour of recording: performance, followed by explanations from the musicians, followed by questions by the two of us, and then another song. Rinse and repeat. I know that Sharyn and I both could have sat there for the rest of the afternoon, but of course the musicians had their limits and they had to go.

Before we left, and what should not have surprised me, she insisted on purchasing the man's drum. Keep in mind that this was not one that was put aside for such a sale, but the very one that the musician had been performing on for all that time. After purchasing one copy of each of their albums and a small flute, we headed off to finally begin our tour of the museum.

For most people, the idea of walking around a busy museum ground with a gigantic cigar shaped traditional Kenyan drum would be absurd, but Sharyn did this with an aura of confidence. She made you feel embarrassed NOT to be carrying a drum around. However, the security at the museum didn't quite see it this way and made us check our newly obtained instruments at the coat check.

For the next number of hours, we explored every inch of that museum. We stood in the shadow of a gigantic taxidermy giraffe and elephant, joking about our feelings of inadequacy. We had the time of our lives playing with all of the informative games located around the main natural history section. While undoubtedly the games are intended for the five years old and under demographic, that didn't stop us from giggling with glee as we stuck our hand in the 'Guess that mystery item' game. Somewhere in the big 'I Was Here' museum guestbook you will find the name Sharyn Poole scribbled in with a red crayon

Our conversation was continuous as we found endless inspiration around us. We discussed Africa being the cradle of Humanity as we passed the section on evolution. We debated what exactly the implications of the title 'Shree' means for an Indian Guru. I recall us both laughing together as we mocked some of the questionable exhibits, and standing in awe of the section of witchcraft artifacts on display. We discussed the myriad of potential meanings found in the section of abstract student art and both fought to contain our yawns as we meandered through the less than enthralling ornithology section. We covered every square inch of that place and left no stone unturned. A productive day to say the least.

After such efforts we found ourselves sitting at a table in the shade, sipping a cool soda and resting our weary muscles. (Side note: I don't know what it says about her or me, but there is something not right about the 25 year old appearing to be more exhausted than the other three score plus a few).

But I digress. As was often the case with Sharyn, the conversation soon turned to CES and related business. There is no doubt to anyone that Sharyn cared deeply for CES and the work being done, and that her heart and soul were deeply woven into the program. During the weeks that she had been with me in Kakamega she spent countless time and energy working at the Divine Providence Orphanage. It was as though she was only able to find her own peace when she was amongst those young children of such disadvantaged background.

She did not limit herself to just the orphanage. Sharyn was very much involved with all of the events and activities taking place during her visit. One day she might be trekking out to one of our more remote schools to pay a visit, arriving back in Kakamega just in time to be present at the CES Peace Run organizing meeting. Her energy was rivalled only by her spirit.

I had heard legendary stories about Sharyn. About the time she rescued a CES student who had been lured from Eshitari SS and smuggled off to be married to an older man in another village. Sharyn mobilized the school officials and the police along with the Kenya Red Cross to find this girl and bring her back to finish her education. I knew the story about her attending the Principal's office at Ngara Girls HS in Nairobi, demanding to know why two CES students were not in class. And there was the time she took a special trip to Thika by *matatu* to advocate for a CES student at Mary Hill HS. I must say I was in awe of this amazing woman.

It was at the CES Peace Run final ceremony that her 'badditude' really came to light. As I was running around like a chicken with it's head cut off and trying to organize the afternoon's program, I can remember attempting to play the 'pay reverence to your elders' card on her by telling her to stay in her seat.

"You look tired. Just relax here," I said.

"Forget that, where can I help?" she shot back, digging in.

Accepting the inevitability of it all, I suggested that she might go and organize the 200 plus CES School students scattered in the park. Off she went with a mission in hand, and thirty minutes later I found the unified group waiting for me, Sharyn in front.

By this point tasty samosas had arrived and we were both stirring our coffee. I could see that the sun was beginning to set behind the museum, reminding me just how long we had been sitting at the café. Our conversation had turned to the future and we began discussing potential paths forward for CES.

As I had just finished a number of months in Kenya and she had traveled there on numerous occasions, we were both excited to share our experiences and how we thought these could push CES forward. We agreed on many items, disagreed on others, while dreaming up what could be possible for CES in the coming years.

And that is what should be done to ensure that the spirit of Sharyn carries on. I can almost see the look that she would give me or anyone else should we even attempt to pause the CES program for a moment due to her passing. She saw things as bigger than her, knowing full well that she was just one cog in a mechanism of greatness. This is what she embraced on a daily basis and showed it through her actions.

As for anyone reading this, I suggest that you get back to work. It's what Sharyn would have demanded.

Road to Heaven

The road to heaven took an unexpected turn
A profound, life changing encounter
By divine appointment she arrived in Kenya
Just a little before it was time to move on.

Four journeys, beautiful expressions of love in action
An unrelenting fight to alleviate poverty
Confirming her calling, destiny discovered.

Unbowed by the crushing weight of poverty
On higher ground, renewing vows of friendship
Free from a disenchanted and brutalized world
She found her place where body and soul connect.

Her adopted girls a crown of beauty
Orphans called her "mommy", gift from God
She saw them through different eyes
Diamonds, shining like stars in the night
Beauty untarnished by whims of prejudice
Each a pearl more precious than rubies.

Finding new joy, her life was no sacrifice at all
Driven by a constant desire to lift up the needy
She identified with the misfortunes of others
Believed life could be better.

"I must go back, I will go back to Kenya"

The road to heaven took her one last time
To her beloved children.

Under the Acacia Tree Anthology
07/2013

DAMN THOSE JIGGERS

by Senem Ozkin - CES Volunteer to Kenya (July 2016)

Mzungu says: This section talks about jiggers – defined as a 'tiny mite whose parasitic larvae live on or under the skin of warm-blooded animals, where they cause irritation and dermatitis and sometimes transmit scrub typhus'.

CES Canada with the CES Alumnus and ACCES have as of this time of writing (August 2016) completed three Jiggers campaigns in Navakholo sub-County of western Kenya. During a recent visit by Canadian volunteers Renee Rerup, Dennis White, Senem Ozkin and Michael Frederiksen, the team had the privilege of 'lending a hand' at Lusumu Primary School. The following story relates the deep feelings felt by Senem where she writes:

By all appearances, it was just another Wednesday on the school ground; the primary school students playing and chasing one another in the field, a trail of happy screams behind them; and, the secondary school students listening attentively to the teacher in their outdoor class despite the noise of their younger counterparts.

But it was not just any ordinary Wednesday. Shortly after the children's play was done, some of the boys and girls were asked to line up and register; the third jiggers campaign was ready to commence. And no amount of Google research could have prepared the Canadian delegation of CES visitors for this important event held July 6, 2016.

Once the kids were registered, they took their seats on wooden benches not unlike the bleachers at football games in North America. They were each given a piece of soap and asked to wait until a basin full of warm water could be brought to them so they could have their feet washed. They waited patiently and without a trace of anxiety about the painful procedure they were about to undergo.

Even when the time came for the sharp razorblades that would cut out the affected parts of their feet, it was rare to hear a cry or to even see a grimace of pain on the kids' faces. They sat without any sign that they were worried, scared, or angry for having to go through such an ordeal. It was as though they were sitting to have school pictures taken. For them, the jiggers making themselves a home in their feet was a natural part of life.

It is easy to take for granted all the rights and privileges we have as Canadians and it is also easy, in the face of those who struggle for a fraction of the freedoms we enjoy, to appreciate what we have, at least on a temporary basis. But witnessing what happened at the jiggers campaign went far beyond appreciating that we, in Canada, do not have such problems. The demeanour of these kids, their courage in the face of impending pain and knowing this would likely not be the first or only jiggers campaign they would have to resort to for help was astounding. It signalled something far more tragic: a loss of innocence. It was as though they were resigned to the fact this was their fate.

The Constitution of Kenya guarantees children the right to basic education; whether that right is exercisable is a topic for another day. But what the Constitution does not speak to is the manner in which that education will be obtained. It says nothing about whether children are guaranteed to have their basic needs met – to have shoes on their feet, to be free of things like jiggers – so that they can focus solely and exclusively on their learning. It does not guarantee that they will be allowed to act like children, to run around carefree, to play with their mates, to complain and be coddled when they are feeling under the weather, let alone when they have fleas in their extremities.

After dozens of kids, ranging in age from approximately 12 months to 12 years old, went through the process of being de-jiggered, their feet were soaked in sodium bicarbonate to close up their wounds, and on they went, many of them without shoes to their homes. If only we had a pair of shoes or even flip-flops to ease the pain a little bit.

And so after eight hours of concentrated work without a break the jiggers campaign came to a close. Facing the reality of leaving these kids behind and wondering how these brave little souls handled themselves in such a grown-up way was almost too much to comprehend. What could we do to give them back the innocence? So little really when compared to what they gave us.

Shoeless One

Run fast, run hard shoeless one
bruised feet burned by the scorching sun
run on dear child, still time for fun
though attacked by Jiggers

Don't cry out shoeless one
bear the pain just like the other one
who just like you has never won
a day free from Jiggers

Shoeless one I feel your presence
razor cuts deep, a pain immense
strength and courage your only defence
to combat Jiggers

Shoeless one you passed the test
laugh and smile just like the rest
I watch you leave, I am blest
sweet Jesus free from Jiggers

Under the Acacia Tree Anthology
07/2016

IN THE FOOTSTEPS OF PROFESSOR WANGARI MAATHAI

by Michael Frederiksen

Mzungu says: In 2012 CES students planted 600 fresh saplings in the red iron soil of Western Kenya. Was this an exercise in futility or did it somehow make a difference?

Kakamega is Kenya's tenth largest city. Poverty and unemployment abound. The incidence of HIV/AIDS is high and those youth orphaned as a result are most likely not attending school. Many people live in mud huts and shelters with rough galvanized-tin roofs. There is suffering here and there is also pride. People eke out a living hoping to obtain a meal a day – not always guaranteed.

This is a part of Kenya one must experience to understand even a little of the nation's challenges. There are pressures on the environment because of climate change, unpredictable rain patterns and indiscriminate cutting of trees for firewood. Trees are not replaced. Twenty or more years of growth are wiped out in a single day. Scientists predict an environmental disaster will happen if changes do not occur.

March 2012 – tenth visit to Kakamega. I once again experienced the joy of interacting with CES students. There was a wonderful sense of celebration as we heard the girls' choir at Bishop Sulumeti HS and the singing of the Kenyan anthem at Friends Namirama Girls' SS. Students at each location received the tree plants CES had provided for the event.

They heard the story of Professor Wangari Maathai who had sacrificed her life and career for the cause of a green environment, and how she had been the first African woman to receive the Nobel Peace Prize. Anticipation was building as instructions on soil preparation and planting were given. Now it was their turn to do something – to make a difference.

It was mid-morning and the sun was already hot. An advance team had gone ahead with picks to break the hard ground. Students lined up with plants to drop into the holes. In an amazing show of strength they carried buckets of water on their backs. They gave the young saplings a drink of water and carefully smoothed the dirt over the tiny plant. Each tree was planted in memory of someone else who had helped them in their life journey.

And yes, I planted a tree in Kenya. Tears were close to the surface as I joined this beautiful line up of students. It was a magical moment where CES students displayed a resolve to do something to make their community stronger. They were learning that in giving there is great joy.

Principal Stella Chitechi (Bishop Sulumeti Girls HS) taught me a lesson in humility. Water had to be carried to the site where the trees were being planted. By hand pump I filled up a 10L jug of water that clearly ended up too heavy for me to carry the half kilometre required. Mdme Principal, always gracious in her words, indicated that she thought if I could just find a rope it would be easy to strap the plastic jug onto my back and my legs would do the rest. "Easy for you to say", I told her. With that Stella picked up the jug, placed it on her head and left without a word. Later she explained that I was not to feel badly as she had been doing this from the time she was a little girl in the village.

While at Namirama Girls HS, another lesson, not so much in humility but more in developing character. A blazing sun made it hard for *mzungu* to plant and take photos at the same time. "Take my picture…take my picture…over here." Soon I was perspiring and nearly ready to keel over as dehydration began its attack. Melvin Wafula, then in Form 2, wanted a photo planting her tree. Enough was enough and I was done. Then the encouragement I shall always remember, "*Mzungu, mzungu…*you must persevere *mzungu*". That was all I needed to take at least one more photograph that day.

Living a life of service for others is a tough concept in a world where every ounce of energy is expended on self-preservation. Yet, it is still possible, particularly when partnership and teamwork prevail. One sows, another waters and miracles begin to happen. What took place in Kakamega was a small example of what is possible the world over. Reforestation and tree planting are important to sustain the environment. Volunteering to do it is equally important. The end result is a feeling of hope that rises from the human heart that says, "I can make a difference – I can do something to change my world."

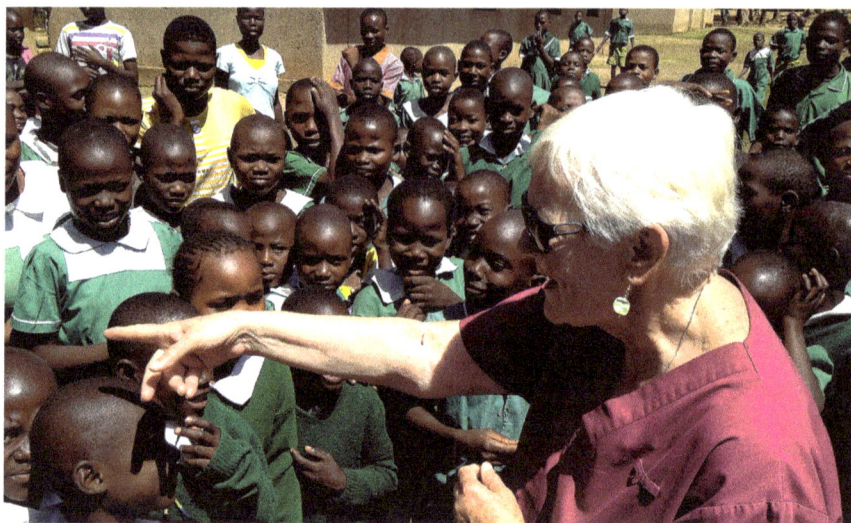

Sharyn Poole, CES volunteer from Rosseau, Ontario, was a beloved mother figure to many of our orphaned youth. Here, on one of her many visits to Kenya, she interacts with students at Navakholo Primary School. Sharyn called Kenya her "second home" and it was there she passed away in 2013. Her life was an inspiration to all who knew her.

Twenty-seven elite Kenyan marathon runners participated in a CES-sponsored Peace Run. It was a world-first event that promoted the need for peaceful federal elections in 2013. Here CES students lead a parade to Muliro Gardens, a public park in the city of Kakamega where 2,000 people have gathered for a unity and peace rally.

CES Canada Director Tom Conant spent a full year volunteering in Kenya. He provided leadership and coordination for the 2013 CES Run-for-Peace, a De-Worming initiative involving 50,000 students, a library project at Bishop Sulumeti Secondary School, and a hydro-electric project at Musaga SS. Popular with young people of all ages, here Tom enjoys time with some children from Navakholo.

Sandy Guthrie, CES volunteer from Thunder Bay, Ontario, Canada was the unstoppable force who drove the launch of the Canada Day Run in 2011. This annual CES tradition brings students together from all CES-supported schools. Here Sandy leads a group of girls in their pre-run stretching exercises.

The Canada Day Run event offers prizes of gently-worn running shoes to each participant. These are donated by Canadian running enthusiasts and New Balance, along with the assistance and support of the Canada Running Series. Here, CES graduates Melvin Wafula (left) and Viewtone Achaga help organize the distribution of athletic shoes.

The Canada Day Run in Kenya was established in 2011. It celebrates the friendship between Canada and Kenya, bringing CES students together for a day of sports and inspiration. Here the Girls 5K race gets off to a good start. Some run barefoot, eager to win for their school.

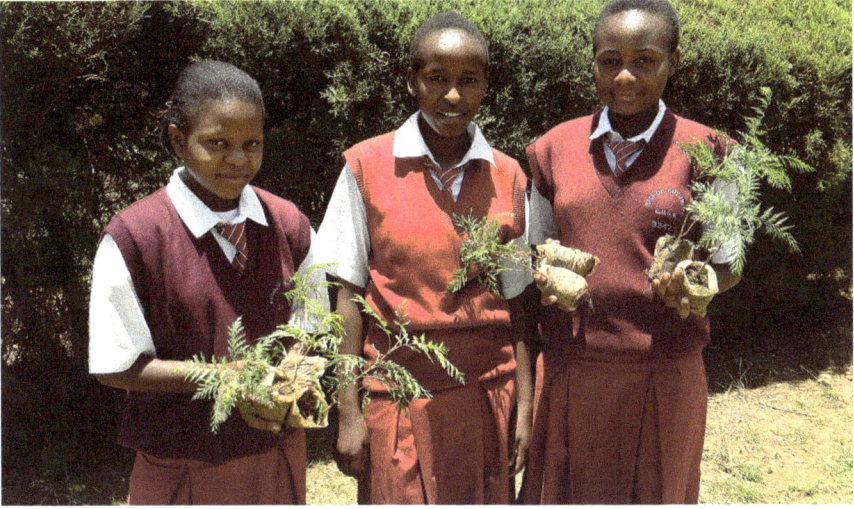

Forests in Kenya are being depleted at an alarming rate. CES programs also focus on the importance of students volunteering and protecting their environment. Here CES Kenya students from Bishop Sulumeti Girls HS participate in a tree-planting project. Three such initiatives have resulted in about 3,000 trees being planted.

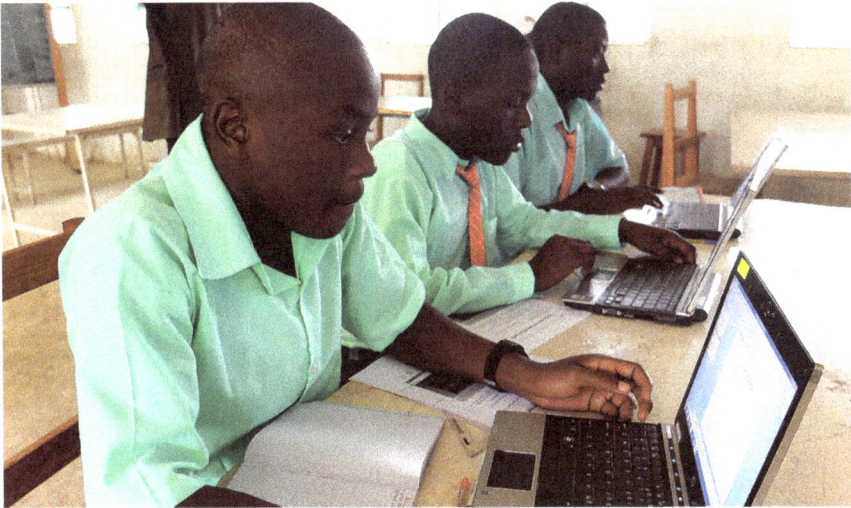

The CES mobile computer lab project involved 330 students in 25 schools. Three teachers utilized thirty computers to provide 110 hours of instruction in basic computer skills. An all-important certificate was awarded to those who completed the program. Funding for this project was through The Peter Cundill Foundation.

CHAPTER 11:
Race Against Time

"There is a price to every achievement"

Kenyan proverb

by Tom Conant, CES Director and Project Coordinator

Mzungu says: The following story may never be duplicated and is among the most historic of all athletic events ever to be held in Kenya. Thanks to CES Canada Program Coordinator Tom Conant and CES Sports Ambassador Gilbert Kiptoo for their roles in creating a greater awareness of peace and reconciliation in Kenya and beyond.

CES KENYA PEACE RUN – FEBRUARY 10, 2013

CES Canada/Kenya initiated a Peace Run in rural western Kenya to create national awareness of the need for peace and reconciliation in the upcoming 2013 Kenyan elections. This event made a clear statement that peaceful elections are essential for the nation's continued health and forward growth.

The Peace Run was timely and very important in the life of Kenya. During the previous election of 2007, violence tore the nation apart, leaving 1,000 dead and 300,000 people displaced from their homes. The cry of 'never again' was heard across the nation, a desperate plea for peace and unity for Kenyans as they went to the polls on March 4, 2013.

The CES Kenya Peace Run took place on February 10, 2013. Organized by CES Sports Ambassador and elite runner Gilbert Kiptoo, twenty-six male and female athletes ran distances from 14 to 24 km in pairs. Each ran a portion of the overall distance of 140 km, a distance equal to three marathons. Along the way there were water points and baton handoff locations set up along the ten (10) leg run.

The run started at Kipsigis County Council offices, along the Kericho/ Kisumu Hwy, continuing past Kericho and around Kisumu, up the Nandi Hills Escarpment and ending at Muliro Gardens in Kakamega. The CES Kenya Peace Run covered territory that was hardest hit by the 2007 violence. It was intended to be a vivid reminder that respect for human life and freedoms is paramount in a democratic society. The Peace Run brought communities and people together, to remind them that peace is the only way to growth and prosperity.

Local authorities, police services, St John Ambulance paramedics, Kenya sports organizations and the media were involved. Other key players included the Physical Education Department at MMUST (Masinde Muliro University of Science and Technology), AK (Athletics Kenya) officials as well as a number of municipal and district leaders, including the IEBC (Independent Electoral and Boundaries Commission).

2,000 supporters from the Kakamega community as well as CES schools and students throughout the area gathered at Muliro Gardens for an awards ceremony in Kakamega. School choirs from Shikoti Girls, Bishop Sulumeti Girls and Namirama Girls sang as the streets were filled with joyful young people marching for the cause of peace.

The good news is that over the past two elections there has not been nearly the violence and conflict experienced in 2007. CES Canada is proud to be a part of ground breaking Kenyan history. The message from this unique event was seen and heard by an estimated 30,000 people along the route from Kericho to Kakamega.

The story as told by Peace Run Coordinator Tom Conant:

It was only 7am, CES Patron Malik Khaemba was already there as I arrived at our Sheywe base of operations. After months of planning, countless meetings, and an incredible amount of coordination we were ready to make the idea of a run for peace a reality. Twenty six runners, officials and dozens of volunteers were expected by mid-morning. Final arrangements, briefings and then we would be on our way. But first there were race materials to be organized and distributed, teams to be coordinated, final plans to be made, and of course the last minute crises to deal with. For a number of hours it all seemed like a blur. Everyone had their personal agenda and questions, and in the middle of it all was the steering committee trying to take charge. It was 'controlled chaos', with an added sense of confusion and disorder. By early afternoon the buses were packed and the only thing left to do was to get ourselves to Kericho.

A convoy of vehicles left Kakamega for the 138 km drive. Considering the early morning ahead of us, we all wanted to get there as soon as possible. What was of particular interest was to finally see what the race course looked like. If I hadn't seen them do it with my own eyes I would have never believed that a group of people could run that distance over such tough terrain. We arrived at Kericho, set our watches and coordinated details. After a small dinner we were in our rooms by 9:00 o'clock. With a million things running through my mind, it was well into the night before I finally was able to get some sleep.

Sunday, February 10 – 5am I woke alert and read to go! No matter what, a race was going to be run this day and there was no stopping it. If we had forgotten anything it was too late and we would just have to deal with things as they emerged. In the early morning darkness, we felt the cold as we made our way to the pre-arranged starting spot. Funny how no matter how much one plans for something, there inevitably is a level of uncertainty during implementation. Today was no exception. A flurry of activity was going on as people were arriving, vehicles were organized, and last minute preparations were being made. I remember just standing there watching it all transpire, wondering if this would be the theme for the whole day.

That morning I learned that the idea of 'Kenyan time' does not pertain to marathon runners. These are people whose whole livelihood revolves around punctuality. At exactly 6:00 a.m. I was talking with some other officials about race related matters. Paul Kimugul, official starter and professional runner called the runners to the starting line. This was history in the making. Never before had Kenya seen a race that covered over three marathons. And what was even more amazing was that not one ran for personal glory – it was all about Kenya and the hope that peace and unity would prevail in the upcoming elections.

"3...2...1...GO!" and with that Philip Kiptoo and Thomas Kosgei took off down the road ... I mean they were gone as soon as they began, literally flying down the street. As they disappeared into the early morning darkness a sense of urgency came across the entire convoy team. I jumped into the bed of the pickup truck with camera in hand and we were the first to take off after the runners.

I have always thought it impossible to be cold in Kenya; that is, until I found myself just before dawn in the back of a pick-up truck, barreling down the highway. "Dear God it was cold!!!!" My breath was right out there visible, like back home on a December's day. My single t-shirt was barely enough to keep in the heat. However, there were bigger fish to fry besides me worrying about any slight discomfort. We had two marathon runners alone on the road with no escort. Let that give you a sense of just how fast these guys are. It took us a bit of driving to finally catch up to them. We took our position maintaining some distance directly in front of them, a position we would try to hold for the next six hours.

Our goal was to bring attention to the message of peace, and there is no doubt we succeeded. Starting in Kericho up front at the head of the pack was a continuous police escort. These officers would tag each other in and out as we passed through different county zones, alternating between motorcycles and jeeps. For much of the race I found them to be somewhat unnecessary, but then when my friends explained just how much violence certain areas had seen in the past, I saw the necessity. Immediately behind the police was the pickup truck. Hitching a ride with me was the official race documenter and three supervisors, all professional marathon athletes. What a blast! There is no better way to see the country than by riding in the bed of a pickup truck as you bump your way down the road, all the while hanging on for dear life.

Behind the pickup were the star athletes, moving at their own pace and who were immediately followed by the official race ambulance hired from Kenya Red Cross. Not only did this vehicle conduct all post-run checkups and deal with any cramping, it also provided an extra source of attention grabbing through the megaphone located on its roof. Following behind were the three transport buses. This included a 14, a 23, as well as a 44-seater bus provided by CES Kenya associate school, St. Mary Goretti Shikoti SS.

While the other vehicles stayed glued to the runners at all times, the three buses worked in tandem to rush ahead in order to set up the cheering squad at the side of the road and at all transition zones. No one wore a seatbelt. All occupants were hanging out of the windows each time they booted past the race pack. In a somewhat 'Mad Max' style, this convoy of peace cruised down the road at a marathon pace. The only remaining member of the convoy was the "Party Wagon Dance Truck". It was somewhere up ahead.

What a scene, twenty-six male and female athletes running in pairs at a truly unbelievable pace to complete the ten legs of the course. It all appeared so effortless. This group of internationally accomplished athletes (1st in the Madrid 42km, 1st in the Melbourne marathon, 2nd in the Gold Coast 42km, 1st in the Singapore Mizuno Wave Run etc. etc.), their achievements had me in awe. How magnificent to have them all together at one event. Draped over their shoulders was the "amani-peace" sash with its beautifully designed CES Kenya Peace Run logo. Instead of a baton or torch, they passed the sash to the athlete waiting to run the next leg. It was like royalty, a regal event as the mantle of authority was handed over.

We survived the cold morning and the sun slowly came up to warm the day. Moving along, our convoy kept the runners between us at all times. It was hard to predict what might happen further down the road. It was still early and pedestrians were just beginning to emerge. For some, their confused faces gave them away; they didn't know what was happening. Luckily, one of the officials riding along in the ambulance decided to utilize the megaphone attached to the vehicle and began to announce what was the meaning of all this.

"It's for peace — for Kenya — go vote — no violence". There was a sense of urgency and like a passionate preacher, the mantra continued. It had only been four years previous where 1000 people had been killed and 300,000 displaced from their homes due to election violence.

The runners continued their run, cars and people waved us along, and we kept on the move. I had one hand gripping the roll bar mounted on the back of the pickup truck I was riding in, while the other hand held the camera at a ready position. The four of us riding in the back of the truck decided to spread the message of election peace by shouting to all those watching, "Kura Kwa Amani!", or "Vote in peace!" When people heard this message and saw the runners in action, a smile would cross their face and they would raise their hands in solidarity. Those early moments were truly spectacular.

As the race progressed, the two vans filled with athletes and officials would rush ahead and set up positions alongside the road. The CES Kenya Peace banner would be displayed in all of its glory and cheers would be pulsating from people as we passed by. This brought much needed energy and encouragement to the runners. Then all would board the bus again and re-join the convoy, waiting for the next opportunity to create another round of encouragement. All along the way the entire running team was sending the message far and wide. Banners waved, shouts of "Amani!!!" sent out to spectators, runners waving as they passed. It was quite a show and an effective conveyer of the message of peace.

Meanwhile, I kept wondering where the huge dance truck was. I had assumed that it would be just ahead of us to draw attention as we brought up the rear. As we approached our first city centre it all came together. The driver had rushed ahead to set up shop right in the middle of this busy area of commerce. For the hour before our arrival, the music was blasting, the MCs were promoting the race, the dancers were grooving and the comedians were doing their thing. "They're coming...they're just down the road", meant the runners were on their way. People had walked from nearby villages and a large crowd was gathering to see this spectacle. The message of peace and unity in the eve of the coming election was clearly out there.

As we rounded the corner past the Tea Hotel and into the centre of Kericho we were greeted by literally thousands of people lining the streets. The crowd was cheering, yelling "Amani!" and "Peace!" We were swept up in the excitement. I can only imagine what the runners were thinking, as I doubt they had expected such a welcome. But they powered on and concentrated on their pace as best as they could. The whole convoy was alive with energy. Passing through the crowd, we shouted our own messages of peace to the people. Unrestrained applause, some danced. If there was ever a moment of unity amongst perfect strangers, it was then. Too soon we had left Kericho.

The next few hours were delightful. The roadway was relatively flat as we passed by tea plantations that seemed to touch the horizon. Runners would race down the road, spectators would watch in wonder, we would shout out the message of peace and unity, the runners would hand off the sash to the next pair of athletes, and so on. The ambulance would pick up the runners after their 20 km run and attendants would provide each with water and a massage. Thankfully their medical services were not required.

The sun was now fully awake, reversing the temperature. Frigid cold turned to scorching heat. We all did our best to hang in there. I'm sure we were all thinking that if these athletes were able to run twenty kilometres in such conditions then surely we could manage it while riding in the back of a pickup truck. Things were peaceful and we were all content.

Then we arrived at Kisumu and all craziness broke loose. At the outskirts we were joined by the local police force. With two motorcycles and a police jeep to act as an escort we entered the city. But no matter how many police we had and no matter how much we tried to keep the roads open, we were entering the third largest city in Kenya. And now we were attempting to run through one of its busiest parts. Things were undoubtedly going to get messy, and messy they were. Traffic was thick as molasses, with cars coming from all directions and honking their horns in an endless concert. The Kibuye Market was alive with people selling their goods.

Police did their best to stay ahead of the runners and move traffic out of the way. But there was only so much they could do with no traffic lights and an endless stream of cars. At one point I watched helplessly as our convoy became trapped behind some bloke who unsuccessfully tried to merge in front of us, blocking the entire convoy. This left our runners, Gilbert Kiptoo and Ruben Kosgei no choice but to forge on ahead without us. Luckily there were two police motorcycles in our convoy that were able to snake their way through the chaos and stay with the runners. We bullied our way through the crowded streets, got onto Oginga Odinga Road and eventually managed to catch up to take our respective positions once again. We all breathed a sigh of relief as we left Kisumu. We were back to relatively open roads, at least roads we could control.

I imagine the runners were feeling anything but relief as they faced what was arguably the hardest part of the entire course. Now that they had survived the madness of downtown Kisumu, the athletes were staring at kilometre after kilometre of steep incline road all the way up to the highlands of the Rift Valley. The formidable Nandi Escarpment lay ahead. But did they slow down at all? No. Did they at any point complain? Never. After an ungodly number of kilometres forging ahead up the fifteen degree incline they only once asked for water. I can't explain it any other way, these runners were superheroes in their own right.

It was at this point I had to leave the convoy and get myself to Muliro Gardens to help coordinate the final events of the day. For me this was the part I had worried about the most. I was expecting at least a hundred students and teachers to descend on the Gardens for the final ceremony. I had no idea how the day was progressing as my phone's battery had died many hours prior. Boarding one of the vans I was rushed up the Kisumu - Kakamega Hwy through the low mountain ranges past the Crying Stone of Maragoli and finally to Kakamega.

The next hour and a half of my life was another example of "controlled chaos". I arrived at the Muliro Gardens with CES Kenya students and teachers already waiting for their marching orders. There were even more en route. Not only that, the 100 strong Scout troop, who were to act as the guard of honour had just arrived. They were in full regalia and marching style; it was one of the most intimidating displays of discipline I have seen in a long time.

I realized that not only were we waiting for the Provincial Commissioner to arrive at the Gardens, we also had no idea where the dance truck was. It was absolutely essential to the parade. Students were getting restless as I tried to mobilize the teachers to in turn organize the students. Running around between people, calling all necessary actors, I knew in order for the final ceremony to go off in a good way that timing had to be perfect. Considering that I was using a borrowed phone to ascertain the dance truck's location, it would be an understatement to say that tensions were high. I apologize now to everyone whom I might have been a bit short with, but sometimes you've got to be.

Finally, things came together as we mobilized the students to a pre-arranged location. The dance truck arrived and the students got into position behind it. No rain on this parade. I had no idea of what to expect, but I took comfort in the fact that the arrow of time will always move forward and no matter what, this would end eventually. We were joined by a traditional Kenyan sukuti band, dressed in full costumes with drums in hand. The CES lead girls held the large "Amani Peace" banner and we were ready to hit the streets of Kakamega.

I must be extremely naive, for I actually believed that when we asked 200 students to remain in two straight lines with energetic sukuti music pulsating, they would actually listen to us. As one might guess would be the case, as soon as the parade began, the two lines became a mass of people and the march became a quick dance pace as CES students stormed the streets. A few hundred marchers and dancers quickly morphed into a thousand strong. People joined the party, came alongside and things just took on a life of their own. But as the futility of my efforts became apparent, I accepted that when in Rome I should simply just do what Romans do. No need to panic. That, plus I decided that if the teachers didn't care, then neither should I. It can be hard sometimes to let go of our cultural conceptions of how things should be done. This seemingly unorganized and almost rampaging parade went against all notions of order I had grown up with; and yet, this is exactly how things are done here. And you know what? I can say that I'm glad this was the case.

Students and hangers on charged through the streets, singing, dancing and shuffling en mass. I could see it in the eyes of each girl and boy – all their months of pent up frustration with authoritative order was finally to be expelled and released onto the streets of Kakamega. All I had asked them to do before we began the Peace March was to stay safe and to spread the message of peace and unity to the people they passed. They grooved through the streets, shaking hands with the people, singing along with the music, laughing and cheering as the sukuti band led them on. People emerged from buildings on both sides of the street to see what all of the commotion was about. I have seen a number of these kinds of parades before, but I am confident that Kakamega has NEVER seen anything like this: over two hundred students, plus pedestrian conscripts, shuffling their way along, spreading the message of love and peace to all the people they passed. Never before in my life have I been more proud to be associated with such a group as this.

We arrived at the gardens just in time to see the massive scout troop officially welcome the official Guest of Honour, Mr. Hillary Mibey, Kakamega Central District Commissioner. In a well-organized display, they did a formal marching salute as they passed by the tent and headed on their way. It was at this time that word came that the runners were almost upon us. The MC pumped up the crowd, the music was blasting, and finally the victorious warrior-like athletes all together descended on the Gardens to a large adoring crowd of several thousand awaiting them. They were instant celebrities as they greeted the crowd fondly, the crowd reciprocated in kind. The runners then momentarily left to be treated in the first aid tent.

Bishop Sulumeti SS and St Mary Goretti HS at Shikoti did a fantastic job entertaining the crowd, their choirs taking turns singing and dancing. Eventually, when the athletes were all treated and comfortable, the official presentations began. Certificates of Appreciation were given to each of the athletes and officials by the District Commissioner.

The final ceremony began. It was a wonderful way to end the day with formal speeches and words of hope. Malik Khaemba, CES Kenya Patron and Chairman Ben Udoto were joined by government officials, athletes and organizers of the event to say a few words about 'Peace'. Everyone listening was in agreement that the message was important and very much needed in the weeks before the election. People were content, the crowd was attentive, and it all concluded in a celebration of unity. An aura of peace surrounded us – a perfect end to an extraordinary day.

All great things start as a simple idea, a creative action to enable bigger and better things. While it is impossible to say exactly what kind of impact the CES 2013 Kenya Peace Run had on the people that bore witness to it, I think it safe to say that the message of peace and unity was spread far and wide.

What happened in Western Kenya on February 10, 2013 was truly historic. There will never be a day quite like it.

Part IV

Hope is Contagious

CHAPTER 12:

Oasis of Learning

"If you want to go fast, go alone.
If you want to go far, go together"

Kenyan proverb

Mzungu says: Oasis of Learning was a phrase used by CES President Michael Frederiksen as he greeted the student body at Bishop Sulumeti Girls HS for the first time in 2012. It is now the name of the Learning Resource Centre and is dedicated to CES Canada volunteer Tom Conant, the driving force to renew and revitalize the school's Library.

Jane CHELOTI
Principal, Bishop Sulumeti Girls Secondary School

There are some cultures in Kenya where they'd rather the girls were being prepared for marriage, rather than being educated. This idea of girls going to school is something new and sometimes it's inconveniencing to some families, who want the girls to take care of the home and the young ones and all. Often the girls are even delayed and held back as the boys go to school.

Things are changing now. The government policy is, if you are found with a child at home, it is a problem. So now, parents are being forced to take the children to school, but it has been hard for them. If a day school, girls are still kept home from school. Sometimes when a mother wants to go somewhere, she will say to the girl, "Now today don't go to school, stay with the young ones as I go to do this business."

So girls have real challenges in their education, not the least of which is their menstrual cycle. They stay at home and miss valuable time. They often do not know what is happening in their bodies and don't know how to take care of themselves. They don't have the feminine pads, and are at a disadvantage. CES has been helping with this. Pads and soap are given give the girls along with some counselling and education. It helps so that they stay in school and that they feel comfortable. No longer withdrawn or embarrassed, they remain in school and do much better in their exams.

Betty MAKONA
Teacher, CES representative, BSGHS

Mzungu asks, "What are the issues affecting girls attending school?"

Barriers are many. Paying school fees is one. Money is something they will not have and even if fees are paid, you know there are a few other things that come up. And here in Kakamega, we have other problems including political turmoil. There are communities where girls are normally circumcised, although that doesn't happen here so much. Circumcision is also referred to as FGM (female genital mutilation). When that happens, those girls are supposed to get married off immediately. They have no chance to complete their education.

Moreover, there are other girls who get pregnant along the way and sometimes they can't go on with their education as they have this burden of the child. They have to take care of that baby according to the mainstream culture. Although nowadays that practice is wearing off, many girls are still not returning to school.

In fact, we see big changes in that the girls are taking over and being more assertive. At least they're trying and of late they have really been supported. People are noticing that more girls are attending school. It's organizations like CES and others that are now supporting the girls. We are starting to have the girls coming up in society and they're getting more confident.

I was at a function for mixed schools recently. And somebody was requesting for a volunteer to pray. The ones who responded were girls, and not the boys. Boys are starting to get comfortable, sitting back, watching the girls do things. We are very happy about what is happening so far. We are starting to see the impact, but there are other times girls are bullied by the boys.

Mzungu asks, "Why is the extra expense of boarding school worthwhile,
if the money could be saved from the students living at home?"

If the students are going home at the end of the school day, there are problems with the distance from school to home, and also the changing weather. It rains almost daily in Kakamega. Day scholars are very disadvantaged because they have to walk home in the evening, and worrying about being caught in the rain. So they will want to run off before the rains. The roads are also very muddy and hard to manage.

Here at Bishop Sulumeti, our boarding school helps them a lot. In other places boarding schools are often for problematic children facing different challenges. Here it is better, and if you want the best education for your child it is here at a boarding school.

Yet there are other negative effects, like the contact between the parent and the child is really cut off. But most of the time, students are in school and they know that in a short while they will be home.

There are many private schools here. Most of them are based on religious affiliation. They generally do better than the public schools. Of course, we have big public schools that are established and they do well. But we have others in the rural areas that don't do as well. Private schools want to attract students by achieving good performance. They work so hard to ensure that they attract the best students. And most of them don't have any crowded classes.

In public schools, the major problem is the high student population. The teacher student ratio is high and sometimes children get lost in the crowd. But in private schools the ratio is more balanced, the class sizes are less and more children are connected to their teachers.

Peninah SHIMULI

CES Sponsored Student at BSGHS

It has been three years since I was in Form 1, and I will soon be in Form 4. I feel good and very happy because my tuition is paid by CES and I don't find myself going home for school fees. I don't miss any lessons because I am always in school and it helps me study. In terms of providing other items like sanitary towels, I say thanks to CES for making me feel comfortable in class. I don't feel ashamed because when I have my periods, I'm not scared.

Mzungu asks, "What about visits by CES staff member Sarah Nabongo?"

For sure when somebody really helps you and then she comes to check how you are, it means that the person really wants good results from you. Sarah really wants to see me excelling. So it means, as much as CES is providing us with school fees, they're not leaving us like that. They come and check on us, so they really want to see us comfortable. And it really shows that they love us. So I feel very good, and by the way in my future, I would like to be a CES alumni too.

After I finish Form 4 I want to go to a Kenyan university like Strathmore University (a private, non-profit university in Nairobi) and study Medicine.

Why I want to do medicine? Because I want to help people. In this world today so many people are getting sick and I want to help them. And besides that, I want to improve my life too. I want to have a comfortable life if I'm working. For example, as a doctor I won't depend on anybody else. I will depend on myself, so I would be able to provide for myself and even support other people who have difficulties paying their school fees. I want to give back something to repay what I have been given in my life.

UNBOWED

Unbowed, against brutal odds
determined to succeed, to make the grade
Untold heretofore, I now share my story
transformed by hope that cannot fade

Unwanted, I long to enter the gates
to learn, to grow, to find my way
Unloved, without even a fifty bob
for books or uniform I cannot pay

Unfounded, the myth that my life
is mired in the muck of misery
Unbelievable, the will to win
to overcome a life of abject poverty

Unbeaten, I rise above my circumstance
that seeks to destroy the heritage that's mine
Undaunted, I regard not the fools that say
that knowledge and learning is a waste of time

Unashamed, I embrace my future boldly
every day with help I persevere
Unavailable to idleness and useless chatter
I perceive the goal to be very near

Unfathomable, the care and love I receive
from friends that bring me hope from above
Unfettered, I now can face the future
my life restored by the power of love

Under the Acacia Tree Anthology
06/2014

CHAPTER 13:
As Iron Sharpens Iron

"Something little is better than something promised"

Kenyan proverb

Mzungu says: At the side wall of the Administration office at Navakholo SS is a large sign, "As iron sharpens iron, so one person sharpens another." Proverbs 27:17. This CES school emphasizes collaboration and group work where students help each other and work together.

Sharon URANDU

Form Four Student, Navakholo SS

Mzungu asks, "How does it feel to know your fees will be covered by CES?"

I have been sponsored by CES since Form One, and I really appreciate the help, because at home my parents could not afford the fees. I have gone through the system and this is my last year. I hope to get the grades that will admit me to the university. I feel so proud because when other students are sent home to collect school fees, I am able to stay in class and I have time to revise my studies. It is a good feeling to know that this burden has been lifted from my shoulders. My only responsibility now is to achieve and do well in my grades.

Aquinas WAMUKOYA
Principal, Friends School Navakholo

Mzungu asks, "What does CES do for students?"

First of all, CES pays for their fees. In addition, students are mentored and counselled and made to feel like they are valued. CES also supplies them with some personal effects, and also, you might say, makes them 'normal'. That feeling of being unable to do anything in life, that feeling of desperateness, that feeling of poverty is gone. The work of CES helps to normalize the students. When they don't have that worry (paying school fees), they will focus their mind on their studies, and focus on a productive life. They don't stress that they will be looked down upon as people who are unable to do anything. People look down on you if you're poor, even if that is not your doing. Of course we have no choice about the family we are born into.

CES also holds seminars, some workshops and regular school visits. They talk to the learners and keep encouraging them, and opening up their minds to opportunities that are available in life. School visits are highly important to the learners. Communications are at close range, addressing individual needs and personal desires and feelings.

CES funds the university costs of high performers fully, and they also subsidize the fees of some who attain lower grades. They also give them equipment like laptops, which are such a good addition to the funding.

Cosmos MASON
Teacher, Navakholo SS

Mzungu notes: As 'mwalimu' (teacher) points to the plaque in the entrance hallway listing each year's top students, he says, "As of now, the top levels that our students have achieved is this group on the wall. The highest is CES sponsored Allan Utumbi from 2014. He has the record for Navakholo SS."

Some of our very best students, listed on the board, wouldn't have had a chance to go that far if we had to go by what their parents had as their inputs. You might ask, "What's different about them if they do not have to worry about fees?" If you look at them, the fact that they actually are there in class is a miracle. Most of them have already achieved many of their goals in life because of their efforts. They wouldn't have made it that far otherwise.

Before they were taken by the CES team, they were having fees problems. They still have that poor family background, and the support that CES provides is actually very important.

Mzungu notices that on a Saturday, what seems to be every student in the school is in the yard under the shelter of some trees, studying in groups. Mzungu is amazed; this doesn't happen where he comes from. So he asks, "How is this possible?" Mwalimu says it's partly because this is a boarding school, not a day school.

As you can see, they're studying hard today, on a Saturday, in groups. Right now, they're preparing for a mathematics contest that's just for our school. You see that the principal is moving around to see how the groups are working. Soon they go back to class for the contest itself. It will be marked. We really want to build that culture for liking mathematics. It is a subject that so many people hate.

This works well in boarding school environments because we can support their self-control around being focused. When they are away from the school, that self control may not be there. Given Kenyan life and home realities, it could be that at a day school, so many of them get alternately hopeful about learning and then pulled down into despair by their home circumstances. But when they are kept within the school they'll keep studying, even on a Saturday. On Sunday they are likely committed to church issues, and soon enough they find that the weekend is over.

By the next day, it will be back to school. So you find that they are equally occupied, meaning that they have little opportunity to be up and down. We hope to keep them focused.

Joseph KULUNDU
Parent and PTA Member, Friends Secondary School Navakholo

I had a son here at Navakholo SS. He was sponsored by CES and he did well. He then joined an agricultural college, passed, and now he wants to continue his studies in agriculture at Jomo Kenyatta University. Surely some student's parents are very poor. When they are sent back home looking for school fees they waste a lot of time being out of class. They arrive home, finding nothing there, they return to school empty handed. And the administration asks them again to go back and as they continue traveling they lose a lot of their education.

With your program, it has assisted them so well that they have always stayed in school throughout to continue learning. I think this is where we should appreciate you very much. The community is not actually well off because they used to take their sugarcane to a sugar factory, which has now collapsed. And parents have no other source of income to let the children stay in school, and they find it difficult to be in school because of lack of fees.

We always ask the students to work hard and the parents also to try and do something about their children being in school all the time. So they bring the school fees bit by bit but at the end some students don't finish. As a result, the family continues to struggle financially, and that of course affects the entire economy of the region. CES students have an added advantage by being sponsored.

Sarah OMANI
Teacher, Navakholo SS

Kenyan and African society in general values boys over girls. They give higher priority to boys than to girls. Many families are struggling economically, so they would rather take their boy child to school at the expense of the girl child. When a family has both boys and girls and they are not able to support them all in school, they would rather educate their boys. So that is the first barrier that girls face.

Some of them do very well academically, especially at the primary level because education is 'kind of free' initially. So they go through primary education, and do very well in the Kenyan Certificate of Primary Education.

But when they are to join high school, most of their parents are not able to raise the finances to take them through high school. Many drop out after Class 8. That becomes a challenge, because when they drop out of school the next thing for them is to get married. And they will get married to people who are also economically poor. So the cycle of poverty continues.

That is why we pray that we get people to support our girl children. That is because when you have empowered a girl-child, when she is able economically, she goes ahead to help others and to support her family. I don't know if it's only in Kenya, but in most of our Kenyan families, if a woman is empowered, it does well. When every child goes to school the community will be much better off.

That's why we pray that many of our girl children get education so that in the future they are able to take care of their families. So when we get such an organization like CES that comes in to support our girls it is very good, because we give a chance to many girls to get an education. And we know that the future of our families is brightened.

What CES is doing is very good for us. What makes it good for girls is that when they are sure someone is paying their fees, they can concentrate on their studies, and therefore they perform well academically.

In Kenya, our education is academically based. If you go through the system and have not passed academically, you may not get the bright future you desire. So for girls to be in school, with somebody paying their fees, they can concentrate on their studies and therefore they excel. CES students are bright and are in position to attend university. We sincerely appreciate this because it is helping our society and our families.

Roselyne NAMUSENDE
Principal, St. Patrick's Ikonyero Mixed SS

CES has been sponsoring our students since 2006. They come from the surrounding area, from poverty-stricken homes; yet they are performing, and they are disciplined. We have seen them move from one level to the other through the hands of CES. And I really appreciate you (CES), because aside from paying the fees for them, CES is also looking at the social needs, and we have had the girls being cared for.

The rest of the students look at the CES students, and really wish to be the one's assisted. And CES has not just left it at the Form Four level, they also take them up for sponsorship even after Form Four.

Mzungu asks, "is there a difference in students who are being sponsored by CES?"

There is a difference because most of the times they are actually in school. Rarely will you find them at home because they are lacking fees. The ones we send home to get fees sometimes don't come back for maybe two or three weeks. So when we can keep students in school, they are able to improve their performance.

Some don't have electricity at home, so CES gives them solar lamps. They know why they are here and why they are being assisted, and usually we remind them that this is a privilege. So when they have that in mind, then they have to make good. CES has provided students and some staff with introduction to computer studies through mobile lab learning. Students end up with a certificate of merit and they are so proud of that accomplishment.

When they find that someone who is not related to them is taking a lot of interest in what they are doing, then they find out that they must be blessed to have the support of this person. When Sarah Nabongo (CES support staff) comes here, she is like a big sister to them, so it means that they have to take her seriously. Her presence has a great impact on our students.

Some people say that now the government is paying everything, but this is not true. The students don't have uniforms, they don't have lunch. The government provides some funding, but it is not timely.

Joan DESIRE
Teacher, CES Representative, St. Patrick's Ikonyero SS

As CES representative for this school, the work involves taking care of the students. CES pays their school fees, but it is not about their fees alone. In addition to ensuring their academic progress, CES is also interested in them as people and they try to give support for their personal problems and needs.

That's important because the majority of the students that are funded by CES come from very desperate and very needy backgrounds, so as much as they need the fees they also need their personal items. In their homes, they have no lighting; sometimes they have no personal effects like soap, pens and pencils. CES also provides mosquito nets, because this is a region with a lot of malaria.

So the CES program goes beyond the payment of their school fees. They also take care of the welfare of the students right from their homes. This includes providing them with solar lamps that can help them to study. You see, at a day school like Ikonyero SS, they study during the day and then they go home and come back the next day. In the school we have facilities that can help them. We have lighting, but when they get to their homes, many of them don't have electricity or even a paraffin lamp. So the CES program provides them with a solar lamp. CES also brings in the soap that they need for cleaning, and what they need for brushing their shoes. That adds to their self confidence.

Even sometimes they go and buy them the uniforms. They may have only one and they're not in good condition, so they take care of that. This is because the personal life of the student also affects their academic results. Unless their self-esteem is taken care of, the fees may not be of much help.

Besides that, they have a counsellor who comes around and talks to the students, to counsel them on their academic performance and the issues that are affecting them. To keep them in school throughout the term, they need to sleep under a mosquito net, so that they don't suffer from malaria. CES is also interested in the health of their students.

As a teacher representative I make sure that they are in school. I find out if they have any family problems that are affecting them, what they may be lacking, and I also guide them in their studies.

I also make them understand that being on the program is such an opportunity to move out of poverty. They now can leave the school and then come back and be helpful to the community where they come from. Basically, that is what I do. I make sure that they are in school every day.

If they are not, I find out why they have not come and if they are being affected by something else that we can assist with.

One problem is that there are so many applicants for the CES program that we don't know how to choose. They'll say, "Madam, please put me in the program. My parents are not able to pay," or "I don't have parents," and you find it is really quite a challenge. We really appreciate even the few that you are helping.

You know that in Kenya there are day schools where most of the students are needy. Some have parents who are dead. The student is orphaned, doesn't really have a home, is trying to rent a small room, is supposed to pay fees; it's really a challenge. So it's difficult to choose which ones to help, because all of the cases are so needy.

As the teacher representative I get asked a lot, "Is there any chance you can consider me for the program?" I get quite a number of requests. The donors in Canada should know that we are reaching out to really needy cases. Let them know that they are really touching hearts.

CHAPTER 14:

Firstborn

"Even dark clouds may pass without rain"

Kenyan Proverb

Mzungu says: In this chapter we have transcriptions of interviews and some text written by the students sponsored by CES. All are trail-blazers in some way – CES' first graduates, who have gone on to build successful careers thanks to the support of CES.

Benjamin Otido WAFULA *BEd, Tambach Teacher's College (2009)*
First among many (900 Grads*2019)
Affectionately called 'Firstborn'

Born in 1986 in Chekata village in Navakholo sub county of Kakamega county, I was the fifth in a family of seven siblings (four sons and three daughters). I grew up in a humble background. My mother, having attained little education was a housewife. My father had no steady employment but he did odd jobs to provide for our basic needs. We lived on a one-acre piece of land and in a single, grass thatched house. I remember very well how we used to survive on one meal a day. I was barely three when my father died and we were left with only our mother to take care of us.

We went to school under tough conditions and far too often were sent away from classes for not paying school fees. We wore torn school uniforms that made us feel uncomfortable. In 2001 I completed the Kenya Certificate of Primary Education, passing with 326 marks out of a total of 500. Unfortunately my mother could not afford to pay school fees for the high school I was selected for, Mukumu Boys HS. I accepted as she pleaded with me to repeat Class 8 so that she could get ready with school fees by the following year.

In 2002 I passed with 395 marks out of a possible 500 on the KCPE. Again I was accepted at Mukumu Boys, again the same story with no school fees. I had just wasted a full year. My mother came to me shedding tears telling me, "I have nothing I can do." Despite passing with good marks, there was no money for fees; I didn't know what I would do.

I felt like a dark cloud was engulfing my future. So I had to stay home for almost half a term. But fortunately she sold the only cow that was providing us with milk. She let it go. Then she took me to a nearby secondary day-school. It was a five kilometre distance and I woke up at 3am each day to walk to school. My dear mother struggled to pay the fees, little by little.

I was overjoyed to meet others who like me promised to work extra hard amid challenges of school fees. Then one day, when I reached Form Four, I had my name called out by the Principal in Assembly telling me, "I want you to go home and bring all your bedding because I want you to stay in this school, as a boarder." I told the principal, "Is this really happening, because my mother can't pay the boarding fees."

The principal replied, "Just go, there is a group of people in Kakamega who want to help bright but needy children in school." So I started boarding at the school. I didn't know it was a group called CES Kenya that had come up with the idea.

I learned later that CES had just opened up operations and was seeking 12 students to support with education scholarships. No one knew much about CES, just that its origins were in Canada. My principal wanted to recommend me and that's what led me to join the CES family of friends.

I proceeded to Form Four with no problem. I was not being sent away for school fees, and I now had enough time to read. With the help of CES Kenya, I had enough time to concentrate on my studies. I did my Kenya Certificate of Secondary school in 2006 and scored a respectable B- grade. In fact, I am happy to say that I was the first CES graduate. The CES Canada

President still calls me 'Firstborn'. CES Kenya partnered with ACCES Kenya to support my college fees. I joined Tambach Teacher Training College to pursue a Primary 1 course, and I graduated in 2009. I came back after finishing training, and started volunteering with CES Kenya.

ACCES Kenya hired me to teach in some of their schools around Kakamega. I taught for three years, and then the contract ended. Those schools were to run privately and then were to be transferred to the government. I looked for another private school and have been teaching around Kakamega at the same time volunteering in the CES office.

I was teaching until 2017 when some schools were merged, and many teachers, me included, lost their jobs. I remembered that if it hadn't been for CES Kenya I don't know what my future would have been, maybe languishing in the village. But actually someone, somewhere noticed that my appetite, my thirst for education was strong.

I decided to go back to my village. I wanted to plant the same seed that CES Canada and CES Kenya planted in me – the need for education for the children. I founded a place where students can come to learn, working together with the community members. I told them, this is what I have learned and what I want to be.

A group of us started up a school in a church, and we teach those children (ages four to twelve) who are allowed to come. I'm still acting as a volunteer teacher. I understand the community where I come from, and I need them to see what I saw about the value of education. I am grateful to the CES Canada/Kenya Directors for giving me such a privilege in life. Were it not for CES I would have dropped out of school and languished in the village. Currently I am proud to be a teacher at Bridge International Academy as I wait for the government to place me in a public school. Previous to that I taught at a special school in Kakamega called Daisy School for the physically challenged.

Apart from the fact that CES pays school fees for us, they also offered us annual conferences at the Sheywe Learning Centre. We were encouraged to press on and take up a higher role in life. We learned about leadership, how to be successful and living healthy lives free from HIV/AIDS.

CES sponsored students started to develop as leaders. Some people sponsored by CES disappeared after they were finished. But we wanted to continue the contact, so we could go on mentoring others who are in high school. We knew that when we came to speak with them, they looked at us as role models. We have a leadership group and now we are part of a big family.

So we decided that if CES invested in us, so we should help too. The hand that gives is blessed. We have leadership at all levels. So we're thinking about where in the future we can bring in other programs to help students.

The CES Alumnus have come together; and, as a group we wish to give back to the community. We have laid down plans that will guide us in achieving our objectives. As the immediate past Chair of the CES Alumnus, I remain in a strong position to help more students to achieve their dreams in life. I personally have a plan of supporting a student achieve his or her dreams in life.

I thank the CES Board members and all the CES volunteers for their inspirations and planting a seed of giving in our hearts. I cannot forget Mr. Khaemba who in 2006 introduced me to his outside world of friends. I met others who were sponsored by CES. These have become some of my best friends. May God grant him good health and long life. It is because of CES that I have a happy life with my family. I lack proper words to express my sincere gratitude, except to say, "May God bless CES Canada /Kenya."

Doris MIROYA *B.Economics (Agriculture) Moi University (2017)*
Entrepreneur Farmer, Agriculture Consultant

I'm a graduate from Moi University with a BSc in Agriculture Economics. My parents died when I was young. My mom passed away first, followed by my dad, so I was raised by my aunt since the time I was in Standard (grade) 6. Then from there I completed Standard 8.

I went to high school, and still my aunt was the one supporting me. In Form 2 I dropped out of school because my aunt was unable to raise my school fees at the national boarding school I was attending.

So I went to a local (day) school in Form 3, and that is when I was picked up by CES. It was my Principal who informed me that I'd been selected by the staff and the board of the school. That was in 2010. I think it was because I was a bright student. From there I completed my high school, and I was the top student in my graduating year.

When I was accepted by Moi University, I asked CES for help. I wasn't sure how I'd raise school fees at university. I applied for a scholarship and I was fortunate to receive such for the entire first year. Since that time I know that friends of Sharyn Poole who I dearly loved and called my 'mommy', continued sponsoring me from Canada. I am so grateful to Fred and Sarah Neal for they have made it possible for me to finish my university studies. I graduated with a degree in agriculture economics. I am glad that CES came in, because I am sure that if it wasn't for them I probably wouldn't have studied after high school.

I am an entrepreneur. I've leased some land in a neighbouring county and that's how I do my tea farming. I also lease some other land in another county, where I do rice farming. I hire people to do the weeding and picking. It's more cost-effective to use manual labour than it is to buy machinery. I also make jewellery, including necklaces, but the market is not so good, so I reduced that to part-time.

This idea goes back to when I was in my third year at Moi University, with the idea of becoming an entrepreneur as a poultry farmer. I didn't have the capital because I was still in school. CES gave me the seed money to carry out my poultry farming. After I got my money back from the venture, I brought back the profits to the office. I thought that maybe if I did that, next time I asked, "Help me, I have this idea", they would respond in my favour.

So when I brought back the money and the profits I heard, "No, you're bringing back the money plus profits, so we know that we can trust you." CES gave me back the cash. Now I know that if I'm going to work, I need to be smart. So, if someone gives me money, I need to give it back with interest. I went ahead and bought a cow for myself to have at my grandmother's place. CES has helped me get on my feet to become what I am today. I have the potential to do something with my life. When I earn something from my rice farm, I put it into my tea farm, and when my tea farm brings in cash, I turn it back into growing rice. So then I realized I could be an entrepreneur.

Alfred Alinda KHAMALA, *BSc, U of Nairobi (2015)*
Specialist, BioTechnology

As the first born of three I was an A student throughout primary school; but circumstances precluded any hope of secondary school. Being a partial orphan, there were simply no school fees available and I was left to languish. An incredible sadness had me in its grip. Luckily, God's favour was on my side. Invited to join a day school, I showed up with nothing and in exchange I was given my school uniform, shoes, and books. I became the highest ever graded student to join St Patrick's Ikonyero SS. I also became the official school Timekeeper.

One year later, CES came into my life. It was Mr. Michael Frederiksen and Mr. Malik Khaemba who saw my potential. I introduced myself as Alfred and it was the CES President who became interested in this young boy in Form 2, sporting eleven subject badges on his school tie. School fee arrears were paid and I landed a scholarship with CES.

My school fees were paid for all through high school. Once again, the glimmer of hope resurfaced. CES is family to me, and I owe my high school to CES. I owe my university degree to CES. It's CES that saw in me potential and to date, everything I do and touch, it is because someone did and touched me from my head to the soles of my feet.

Now with a BSc degree in Biotechnology (University of Nairobi 2015) I am proud to say I can now pay off my student loan and put my kid sister Elizabeth Chalicha through school. She also went through CES sponsorship at Ikonyero SS. Currently I work as a medical representative with a pharmaceutical company. My sister is in 2nd year veterinary medicine and surgery and I pay her fees. I am proud of these baby steps. I am not where I want to be, but am on my way.

I wish to see myself like my CES friends, inspiring lives, helping out all those vulnerable boys and girls within my reach. I want to be a piece of the bigger picture in giving back.

Well, a mere thank you is never enough to describe how I appreciate what you have done for me. CES Kenya and CES Canada is a God send. I am forever grateful to all of you who give towards this charity. It is you that put me through school and helped me put my sister through school. You have made my life better than it used to be.

I have applied for a MSc. Molecular Biology and I have my admission letter to MMUST. I also applied for an International Masters in Agriculture and Nematology to Ghent University in Belgium last week under full scholarship. Whatever my future, I will always say, "Thanks to CES, the best is yet to come."

Allan UTUMBI *BSc Kisii University (2019)*
Computer Technology, Programmer

My name is Allan Utumbi born in 1996 at Mukangu village, Navakholo Sub County in Kakamega County. I am the second born child in a family of seven siblings. My dad is a peasant farmer whose income from farming activities is barely enough to make ends meet. He majors in small scale maize production at a subsistence level.

My biological mother died in 2006 while I was in Standard Four at Mugango PS and aged 10 years. Life became hard since then but we had to accept the will of God. This was not easy as life lost meaning for the five siblings, especially for my youngest sister barely at the age of 2 years. My father could not perform both the father and motherly responsibilities for the home. Since we were in school there was limited time to help him. He was forced to remarry in 2007 to our step mother with whom we have identified for a mum all these years. She has been good to us and made us forget our motherless state. Though she could not wrap the grave from our eyesight, she at least was supportive. She is the mother of two children in our family.

I continued with my education and cleared my primary education in 2010 scoring 326 (B plain mean grade) and joined Navakholo Secondary School. I was offered a placement at a National school at Musingu Boys High School; however, I could not attend for lack of school fees. I joined Navakholo Secondary school, where I did my KCSE in 2014, and where I managed to get a mean grade of A minus.

I was so happy at Navakholo SS, that is until I was sent home to collect school fees. I had done nothing wrong, in fact I stood at the top of my class. By the end of the second term when fees should be cleared for the whole year, I had only paid half. After that I was frequently sent home to collect fees. Often I would leave even before my name was called; I did not wait until the letter U and Utumbi was called out. I was missing more classes daily but kept on coming back to ensure that I maintain the top position in my class.

In the third term that year, a volunteer from CES Kenya visited the school. Madam Hellen Kulundu (CES Kenya Director and Board Member) asked the school administration to identify performing students who might be sponsored. I was identified and she assisted in clearing all my school fees. I had no reason to perform poorly in any test and gradually I improved up to a mean score of an A plain across all the subjects. My family and school community were proud of me and by the time year three approached, CES Kenya carried me the rest of the way. One of the things that helped me in my studies was receiving a solar lamp. Now I could study and do my preps after sundown as there was no electricity where I lived and we could not afford paraffin even to light a candle. All my take home assignments were completed on time.

Life took another channel in my life. I realized I was loved by some good people in Kenya and in Canada. I was encouraged when I attended the annual Canada Day Run for Charity at Masinde Muliro University. There I met other CES sponsored students even more needy than I.

As I interacted with an albino student from Buhayi Secondary, her story impacted me deeply and it changed my perspective towards my academics. How Mourine struggled with intense sun burns but still focused on her academics was amazing, and I could not spare my tears from rolling down my cheeks. I had to go and work even harder, and at the end of the fourth year I scored an A- of 74 points in the KCSE.

CES had organized a mentorship program for those students who had excelled with a mean grade of B+ and above. I was invited to become a Peer Mentor and assistant teacher at Navakholo Secondary. In 2015 I registered at Kisii University for a Bachelor of Science degree program in Computer Science. Prior to that I was invited to apply for a CES scholarship; and after an interview at Sheywe Conference Centre in Kakamega, I was awarded the full scholarship through which my fees and accommodation were paid. I have also trained for a CESCED leadership training program with six other scholars under the mentorship of Faculty Advisor Patricia Makori. The ten unit program provided excellent resources over a year of concentrated study. It was such a happy moment to receive the Leadership Merit Award in the presence of the CES Kenya Board of Directors, Madame Kulundu, Patricia Makori and the CES Canada President Michael Frederiksen.

This leadership program has enabled me to be elected as the chairperson of students from Kakamega County at Kisii University. I am also serving as the vice secretary of the CES Alumnus. As an executive, we have plans to create a group of CES graduates that will make a difference in the lives of others.

Personally, I have learned a lot from my experiences with CES, especially what it means to give back. This has given me a new initiative, to personally support someone in the future. I thank the CES family for making me realize my life goals. I am proud of this fraternity all the time and I always promise never to let the family down. God bless CES Kenya and CES Canada.

With computer science I will be able to do a lot of good things. Most importantly I want to be a engineer dealing with IT networking. That is what I have been doing during my attachment (cooperative education placement). At the same time, I have also enjoyed working as a hardware repair person dealing with computers and infrastructure.

To begin with, computer science is going to help my family a great deal. When I finish this course, I have hopes to get employment, earn a salary and be able to manage many things that my parents cannot afford. Then at the same time, we have a family of eight children who will also not be able to raise their school fees if I don't help them in the future. My salary will enable me to pay school fees for my siblings.

Why network engineering? When you look at computer science, it's so broad like software engineering or IT. Computer science is the mother of those IT courses. You then have options to become a network engineer, a software engineer, and you can also become an IT manager and an overall IT support technologist. There are so many people who have been doing software engineering. This means that the network side has fewer people. That's why it is my interest, because I see it is more marketable than other fields.

Apart from that, when you look at our area here in the village, the network here is a bit slow. You cannot connect to 3G. With network engineering skills I think I can help my community to upgrade to 3G and 4G where you can do your work over the internet very fast.

We can communicate and get information from the internet nowadays. Job markets are being advertised through the internet. By developing or upgrading the internet within the area of rural Navakholo, I will be opening new chances for more people just like CES did for so many of us. Without better internet it is very difficult to communicate. That is why I chose to go for networking.

With Allan as translator, interpreting the answers to my questions in Kiswahili, mzungu asked Allan's parents about changes in their son due to the CES programme:

"There has been a great change, and it's positive. They say that I am doing well since the CES team started to sponsor my education. If I were not given this chance through CES, I would not have managed to come this far, and so I would have ended up in drinking, or being a criminal because of poverty. I would also have given in to other vices due to peer pressure. They told me they were very thankful and were proud of me as their son."

CHAPTER 15:
Courage and Compassion

"After a hardship comes relief"

Kenyan proverb

Mzungu says: The following are two stories about CES graduates who have experienced life-threatening challenges that would make most people give up.

Mwanarabu OTSWANG
Student at Kenya Medical College, Nyahururu

I grew up on a homestead, on a farm. I'm the firstborn in a family of two. My father died when I was quite young. My mother worked to support us. I stayed with my grandmother who is quite elderly and stays at home. I have a sister in Kakamega Primary Specialty School who is mentally incapable.

I went through my primary education at Kakamega Primary School from 2001 to 2008. Throughout those years, I used to fall sick, off and on. An uncle who supported me used to take me to the hospital, and buy the drugs I needed. At the end of each term I performed very well in the exams, so I saw God's doing in my life.

Then in 2008 I got good marks and I was called to a boarding school, but due to lack of funds it was not to be. My next choice was Kakamega Muslim Secondary School.

At that time, my mother used to work as a domestic worker. She was paid on a daily basis and with that little money she could pay my school fees. My uncle used to chip in to pay some fees for me buy some daily necessities. It was in 2010 when my mom died. It was not an easy time. It felt like my world was over.

After the death of my mom the following year in 2011, and while I was in Form Three I became very sick. My uncle spent his time with me, took me to the hospital, and there I was given some expensive drugs. I wondered how these were being paid. I enquired from my uncle, and he opened up to me about my mother. I learned that when I was born, my mother was HIV Positive, and so I was also Positive. You acquire this through your mother, mother-to-child transmission.

My uncle said that he had been taking care of me since Primary school when I was on-off sick. But that was not the end of the world. If I accepted my condition, then I could go for the drugs. I could do better in life and make a change in my family. I asked if I could go to the clinic by myself; and so I went for the big test about my HIV status. I was tested, and the results were shown to be Positive. As a result the drugs were made available to me. The Kenyan government has a program providing Anti Retroviral drugs, (ARV's), to those who have contracted HIV/AIDS.

Then I thought, "I'm the first born. I have a sister who is dependent on me. I don't have a mom. I don't have a dad. I am the only person to make a change in our life of our family." So, I accepted to go for the drugs. By that time my CD4 Count (a measure of white blood cells in a person's bloodstream) was below 200. The doctor told me, it was high time I got started on the ARVs.

I experienced some side effects like vomiting in the morning. Then there were times of headache. I did what I could, I drank a lot of water, and the headache still wasn't going away. But with time it got better and I'm okay right now.

That was in Form Three, 2011. I finished Form Four in 2012 at Kakamega Muslim Secondary School. There I used to perform very well and always at the top position. The Principal came to notice that I had trouble paying my school fees, so he called my uncle who then started paying fees from Form

Two until Form Four. I finished my Form Four in 2012, with a C+, and I had no idea what to do next. Nothing came into my mind.

I thought, I could be an advocate to change the perspective that the community had about HIV/AIDs and help to remove the stigma associated with this disease. I also wanted to work towards a zero mother-to-child transmission. So I told my uncle, I would go for a nursing program. His response, "Can you go for maybe a teaching career?" My reply was, "No, I'm not going to be a teacher, because that is not my passion."

I tried to apply, but it wasn't easy to get a chance at KMTC (Kenya Medical Training College). I applied for the first time and I was not short-listed; I applied for the second time and was not short-listed. Third time, was not short-listed. 2012, 13, 14, 15, 16, 17 – five years of trying. I did not give up.

In the meantime, I started my own business, as I have a talent for hair dressing. So throughout those five years I fixed people's hair. I was paid a daily commission, so I could go and buy some necessities for my grandmother, my sister and I, so that way I could keep on going with life.

I did not get the chance to go and study nursing as I had wanted, but I never lost hope. In 2017, students were applying to KMTC, and I applied once again. There was a lady who guided me toward the courses, and she said there was another brand new program I could take, a Diploma in Health Education and Promotion. It was started because the government wanted to focus on preventative measures rather than curative measures. That's exactly what I wanted – making policies for public health.

I applied with Public Health as my second choice. God answered my prayer in 2017. I was sent a message on my phone saying "Congratulations," and welcoming me to the program. In two weeks' time, I was to report to the College. Now, the amount of money that they wanted was so much. I informed my uncle to say that I had been admitted. He had no idea I had even applied. He thought I was just doing my hairdressing and that was it.

But I was keen and he encouraged me. The funds were due in two weeks' time, and I didn't know if we could raise the amount that KMTC required. Yet I thought it was possible, because if God was giving me this chance, he had a reason.

So I came to the CES office and talked with the Patron, Mr. Khaemba. I told him about everything I needed in order to join the campus. I was called and interviewed. My school fees were paid by CES for the whole year and on top of that there was also accommodation provided for me.

I feel so grateful to be part of the CES family, because right now, CES is like my parents. Your parent will ensure that you get all the basic needs required, are studying, living well, without any major issues to deal with. I think that CES is doing a remarkable job empowering the community through education. I see CES as a stepping stone to a brighter future.

For me, I'm just looking forward. After completing my diploma I can go for a degree course, because with a degree or a Masters in Health Education and Promotion, I can get a well-paying job. I want to give back to society, and I want to be part of the team that is empowering the community, even if it's through education or through advocacy.

Then the second thing is my sister. Oh my God, that's a big burden. I need to see the way forward, how I can help her to make a living since she is mentally handicapped. Then another thing, I'm thinking of helping my guardian uncle and my grandmother get some land somewhere, to build houses so they can live comfortably. Where we're staying now, the land is under a family dispute. So with all I am facing in my life, I think I will have accomplished my mission through God's help. And I am so grateful for what CES Kenya is doing. God bless CES Canada and CES Kenya.

Mzungu asks, "Mwanarabu, what are your thoughts and ideas on how your work will help the community?"

In dealing with HIV, the first thing is to advocate for people who are HIV positive, to encourage them to take their drugs on time as directed by their doctor, and to get them eating a well balanced diet. They also need to avoid unhealthy behaviours, like having so many partners or having sex without protection. They need to put down that mind of thinking that because you got it and didn't know when or how, you want to spread the Aids.

If you do those things, there are minimal chances of you transferring it to your unborn child or even your partner. That is the world that we want, one that is free from the stigma of HIV. There is so much information that the society still needs to know. When you lose perspective around HIV, you can lose hope, but when you are enlightened, you have a little knowledge about that, you see fewer difficulties.

Even now, in Kenya and Africa in general, there is a lot of new infection among the youth ages 13 - 25 years. That's not the way it should be, because we're trying to move into a world that is free of HIV. But the number is growing. It could be the youth that are HIV positive don't have the correct information, or they don't have a chance to talk about it themselves. They can communicate their issues, and then see how the Ministry of Health can assist. It is possible to go in the direction of an HIV-free society.

On a personal level, I am very hopeful about the future for myself and others who are HIV Positive. I volunteer at a support group of adolescents and youth living with HIV. They get together at the Kakamega Referral and Teaching Hospital. We usually meet at the AGM in August each year. I also attend seminars for people living with HIV in Kakamega County. In the various meetings I attend I am recognized as a motivational speaker. I talk to the young people about not being ashamed of taking drugs. Some are either in Primary or Secondary school and they fear being stared at or being asked or being asked why they take these drugs daily. I encourage them to be courageous, to overcome fear and the stigma of HIV. I also tell them it is good to share their status with close friends and relatives, it will make them strong. And when they feel disadvantaged because of their situation they have a shoulder to lean on. My message is always to take their drugs at the prescribed time so that they can achieve a low viral load detection. It is possible to lead a normal life like others who are not HIV positive.

During the 2018 AGM organized by APHIA (Aids Population and Health Integrated Assistance) I participated in a number of discussion groups. We were celebrating those youth and adolescents who had made it to a 'low viral load detection' by taking their drugs as prescribed for them. As motivational speaker, I used the chance to speak to these young people about the need to accept their status and live a happy life. The theme of my talk was, "It *all begins from your inner side*". I shared about my studies and ambitions and encouraged them to follow their dreams. They need to focus on goals in life rather than being discouraged about what other people told them their life would become. It is God that has the final say and we have a lot to do to make all things better.

I reminded them about the story of the donkey that fell into the well, and the farmer who tried to rescue it. The farmer concluded that it was impossible. The donkey was old and the well was dry, so what was the use of helping this poor animal. So the farmer asked his neighbours to come over and help him cover up the well. They all grabbed shovels and began to fill the well with dirt. At first the donkey cried horribly, but then to everyone's amazement, he quieted down and let out some happy brays. With every shovel of dirt that hit his back, the donkey was shaking it off and taking a step up. Pretty soon the donkey stepped up over the well and trotted off.

The moral of the story is that life is going to shovel dirt on you. The trick is to shake it off and be positive. Every adversity can be a stepping stone and the way to get out of the deepest well is by never giving up. What happens to you isn't nearly as important as how you react to it. No matter what you are going through you still have a chance to succeed.

There are many in our Nyahururu community here where I am studying, who are quietly suffering on their own. Some have not even reached the first stage of knowing their status through a simple blood test. They fear the worst and they know something is wrong, but what can they do? My life's work is to help them. It's all about friendship and reaching out, one person at a time. Sitting down over a cup of tea is good. Peer network groups are easy to organize and I will continue to promote these.

As I share my experiences with others, I tell them to let the stones thrown their way pave the road ahead to reach their destiny. I also believe that God has us in his plans. As I prepare for my future work in community health, I pray that my efforts to encourage others who are HIV positive will help many to overcome the challenges they face in life.

Milridah Ayuma OMINDE *BA Education, Moi University (2018)*
Teacher

I studied at Ibinzo Secondary School. When I was in Form Four my dad died and it was at that time CES stepped in strongly to pay my Form Four school fees.

After that I joined Garissa University, specializing in Education (Arts, English and Literature). I was on my own and I went through a lot of hardships. Sometimes I would even starve and I can remember in my 2nd year I missed exams because I had not paid the compulsory fees just to write the exam.

I know you are aware of what happened on April 2, 2015 when Garissa University was attacked by al-Shabab, a Somali based terrorist group. We lost 147 comrades that day. It's with great sorrow and tears that we mourn our friends, my three room mates included. I shall never forget them. May God rest their souls in eternal peace and comfort their families and friends. I thank God for protecting me from the attack. I do not take it for granted. I came out alive and uninjured despite the terror and the trauma. I take this opportunity to thank you for standing with me since the terrorist attack, both financially and through prayers. You are the reason why I smile today.

Maybe I would have deferred my studies due to the huge fee balance that was pending. Who knows? Maybe I would even have given up in studies for I had nowhere to get the money from. I am so grateful today and I celebrate CES for standing with me.

After the attack CES took me back, and gave me full sponsorship towards my education. That was in my second year up to the fourth and they were able to pay for my school fees up to completion of all my courses in August 2018. I want to say I am very grateful because through the school fees they provided, I could also support my younger sister who is in high school. I saved a little and even paid her school fees and do shopping for her.

Since I joined Moi University main campus I was able to learn comfortably. I never starved. I was able to pay for accommodation with no problem and never missed exams because CES was sponsoring me with everything, including my full accommodation. Since then I have finished comfortably without any problem and I'm very grateful.

That meant a lot to me, because when I was in Garissa I used to go through hardships. I was not performing well. But when I went to Moi University through the CES financial assistance, I was able to work hard because I was no longer straining or starving. I was able to concentrate well with no problems, having full time to do my academic work.

The meetings when CES-sponsored students and alumnus get together really helped. We got to know each other. We shared how we were doing and how people were going on after they've been sponsored. Because, you know, some people are not able to complete their studies and others are forced even to defer their studies because they have no means. Many have to work while they are studying, which is very strenuous.

So it helped now that I was given full sponsorship. I was able to concentrate on my studies without doing other things. I was also part of the CES Leadership program and our principal Patricia Makori gave us good advice as we proceeded through. I got to know the others in the group. When we gathered at Sheywe Conference Centre to receive the certificate of completion it was such a joyful time. Everyone was dressed their very best and we all felt special and appreciated for our work.

We exchange contacts and we share ideas throughout the year. Friendships have developed and we are a strong and dedicated group. Our goals are to be active in making the community safer and healthier. For example we have jiggers control programs, hand washing days, and the CES Canada Day Run. We get out to CES Schools and give motivational talks to the students there. It also helps to be part of the Alumni because we get to assist each other, to share ideas and maintain friendships. We have started contributing 100 shillings per month through the CES alumni group, so that by starting January 2019 we want at least to sponsor one student.

About the local Kenyan leadership of CES, they have always been there for us. Sometimes it's just advice we need. It really helps because when for example you have a problem, instead of talking to Michael directly in Canada, we use the Kenyan leadership. It's like an intermediator so that instead of always emailing and calling and all that, we just come to CES Kenya and through Mr Khaemba we share our problems or ideas.

During the last elections (2017) I had the amazing opportunity to serve Kenya as the polling and counting clerk. It helped me learn a lot. I was given the role of queuing clerk. I was put to work in my registered polling station, Ibinzo Primary School. I had a challenge working with my own people because most of them wanted me to put them on the front line; yet, I was there to serve and be faithful to all. The job was very demanding and needed a lot of perseverance since some people were rude and harsh. I had to walk up and down and stand for long time ensuring people remain in queue. I also gave priority to those who were disabled so they would not get so tired. Fortunately it didn't rain on that day.

Despite all the challenges, the job was well done and by the and of the day 619 people had voted in my station, which was 80% of the registered voters. Since it was my polling station, I also had a chance to vote. We counted from 7pm to 2am, so I had to sleep in my polling station till morning. It was a wonderful encounter and a lesson on its own. I liked the job and am ready and willing to work as a clerk or even presiding officer come 2022 if at all I will be given the chance.

Thank you CES for standing with us in prayers. Thank God there was no violence and the voting was done peacefully and in order.

Mzungu says: Garissa University College was attacked by Islamic militants on April 2, 2015, killing 147 people and injuring others. It was later shut down and students who survived had to find another university to attend. CES supported Milridah throughout this time and assisted her in registering at Moi University, Eldoret where she completed her studies.

The following is Milridah's story as told by CES Canada volunteer Karen Dahl, who along with CES Associate Patricia Makori provided crisis counselling and assisted Milridah in the recovery time after the tragedy.

The loss of 147 beautiful young Kenyan university students was horrific. In the early hours of April 2 terrorists entered the gates of Garissa University undetected. A wave of evil swept through the dorms as many were preparing for a day of exams. Those who were gunned down had no chance, most were Christian. By 8am it was all over. The killers detonated their bomb belts taking their own lives.

CES Kenya graduate Milridah Ayuma Ominde was an eyewitness. She describes a morning of confusion and terror. By 5:30 am she was up preparing for the day. Finishing her toiletries she was about to begin her morning prayers and early studies. It was then she heard the shouting, the gunshots, people screaming, and she knew something terrible was happening. She grabbed her cell phone and ran.

"I ran down the stairs from the hostels/dorms to the field which is a distance away. The back of the university compound had not been fenced by wire and I managed to escape through the thorny bush fence. Beyond that was forest and desert. I ran and did not look back. After 15 minutes I found myself on a side street leading to Garissa Town. Other colleagues joined me as we found a bus leaving for Nairobi. As we got to the Tana River border patrol, the Somali bus driver demanded 500 extra shillings. He claimed it was danger pay because of the insecurity. Luckily for me, a friend lent me the money and we continued the eight hour journey to Nairobi."

Milridah spent the next two days at Kenyatta Hospital comforting the injured students who had survived. It was her friend, CES graduate Doris Miroya who was able to contact Milridah. Through Doris, CES Canada was assured that Milridah was safe. A few days later CES Kenya Director Rev. Livingstone Nyanje met with Milridah and invited her to his family home in Nairobi. CES Canada volunteer Karen Dahl had just arrived in Kenya. She and Milridah travelled to Ziwa to spend a few days of rest at the home of CES Sports Ambassador Gilbert Kiptoo.

Gilbert and his gracious wife Sally made us welcome and provided much support and encouragement to Milridah during our stay. This provided the initial opportunity for Milridah to relax and get to know me. I knew the healing process had begun. Life on the farm provided the perfect healthy balance of quiet time for reflection, counselling and links with community activities. Gilbert introduced us at the private school of his brother, James Moiben, where we were given a tour of the facility. A visit to the Zurrie Flower Farm was a refreshing break and so stimulating to the senses. Gilbert and Sally invited us to attend the Passover Feast and service at their church and we had the opportunity to celebrate with them and their church community. It was an evening filled with fellowship, praises and joy.

Milridah spent a few days at her grandmother's shamba. The home is located near to Ibinzo Girls HS and where Doris Miroya's family is from. She was greeted by her pastor and many friends who came to see her. It was a joyful celebration.

Prior to her returning to Canada April 2015, Karen Dahl maintained daily contact with Milridah offering support, encouragement, and continued counselling. She helped Milridah deal with the impact of this event and to utilize some basic coping strategies. Due to the loss of close friends during the attack, Karen also encouraged her to remain connected with her other friends by phone and to consider attending the funerals of her colleagues who lost their lives at Garissa University.

Her closest friend Josephine Onyancha Nyaboke, age 21, was gunned down as she prayed in the Morning Glory chapel with other Christian students. Her other roommates Agnettah Chite and Lucy Nyambura were killed in their beds while sleeping. Milridah did travel to Butere with her friend Florence to join other mourners at the funeral service for Agnettah. She shared that it was sad but that she felt Agnettah was at peace.

Overall, Milridah has been connected with her friends and family and has been coping fairly well. She is the secretary for the youth programme at her church and continues her commitments to her church community. She is staying in the home of her step grandmother and assists with chores and planting vegetables. Milridah has met with CES Patron Malik Khaemba, Chairman Udoto and other board members to provide her account of the Garissa attack.

She has been made aware of the efforts made of the CES family to raise funds to assist her. During the CES Leadership Scholarship interviews, Milridah participated by greeting the candidates and assisting with the ushering of the participants to the interviews. She also addressed the group during the workshops, providing the new graduates with a role model exemplifying strength and courage through the most tragic of events.

Other supports include CES Kenya board member Aziza Rajab. Aziza encouraged Milridah to remain active, continue with her church involvement and volunteer work at the school. In addition, Aziza followed up with a call Karen had made to the Kenya Red Cross inquiring about the counselling services for the Garissa students. Aziza has confirmed that Milridah was on the list for counselling and that a plan was in place to respond to her needs. CES Associate Patricia Makori in her role as a crisis counsellor with the Kenya Red Cross also spent quality time with Milridah.

On Monday April 27th Milridah attended her first counselling session provided by the Red Cross at Kakamega. The students met together and then were divided into small groups with a counsellor facilitating each group. According to Milridah the session was successful. "We were allowed to talk everything about the attack and air out all views", she said afterwards. It was also confirmed that she is to report to Moi University Eldoret in May, 2016.

At this point Milridah had expressed her willingness to apply to attend the Moi University campus to complete her second year of the BA in Education. She had a desire to remain close to home and near her former Ibinzo colleague Doris Miroya who was also willing to provide guidance and support. Milridah would benefit from continued follow-up from CES Kenya for encouragement, problem solving, emotional support, educational guidance and financial assistance to ensure a smooth transition into university life.

Milridah is a soft spoken young woman with incredible strength and courage. Her faith in God is unwavering and her determination to complete her education for the betterment of her younger siblings is powerful.

She is one of six children. Her parents divorced when she was very young and she has never seen or heard from her mother since. Her father and step-mother raised her on the meagre products from the farm. School fees were managed, until her father became ill and died. At that time, she was in Form 3. Her father's death was distressing as she now was a total orphan. This impacted her ability to perform her best in school.

Her focus was further disrupted when her step mother sold the family land and the shamba in which Milridah and her siblings had grown up. Her step mother went with another man and Milridah was left to support herself and two younger siblings. It was at that time that she was assisted by CES Canada with a full scholarship to complete her secondary education. She is concerned for her two younger siblings Melvin Achimbo in Standard

8 and Brancice Aylela, Standard 4. They are both living in separate homes with different relatives. Her father had instilled in Milridah that obtaining an education could improve her life so that she could help her siblings. He told her that he would not always be around.

Milridah is an exceptional young woman, an inspiration to us all. Despite her own situation of fear and uncertainty, she was ministering to and thinking of others. "I was lucky and I thank God He helped me to escape; however, I lost my many friends and three room mates which is very sad for me. I thank CES because they have stood by me and encouraged me. When I was between universities and needed funds to survive I was through CES provided a teaching position at Kakamega Muslim SS. I feel loved and cared for and I will be very happy if you (CES) continue to stand with me so that I can be a strong member of the CES family."

CES Canada and CES Kenya and the entire CES family will do just that. When one suffers we all do, at least in part. It's the least we can do.

CHAPTER 16:
Alumni on the Move

"Your own load is never too heavy to carry"

Kenyan proverb

Mzungu says: This chapter has transcriptions and writings from four CES alumni. These outstanding young graduates we refer to as 'Nation Builders'. Some are graduates of the CES School of Continuing Education (CESCED) Leadership Training program and all have shown strong potential to lead through service to others.

Viewtone ACHAGA
CES Alumnus, student at Nairobi University

I take this opportunity to thank the Almighty God for how far He has brought me. In addition, I thank CES Kenya/Canada for their continued support. I am so grateful and wish to share my story so that at one point or another it may motivate or create in someone else a different perception of life.

I am Viewtone Achaga, a student at the University of Nairobi, pursuing a bachelors degree in Science (BSc). I am part of the CES Alumni and a recipient of a CES leadership scholarship.

I come from a humble family in Kakamega – to be sincere, a large and financially unstable family. Not one of us, including my parents, ever accessed education. I attended primary school immediately after the free primary education was introduced in 2003. Without that, it would have been a different story.

I have encountered all the hardships of life, including going to school without food and attending class dressed in rags. I was determined and never gave up. I maintained a brilliant record in school and was never involved in a disciplinary case. From the time I was admitted, until the completion of Standard Eight, I maintained the highest marks. I was the first student to score above 350 in the KCPE, with a score 365 out of 500 marks.

As I said earlier, I came from a poor family where providing basic needs such as food and clothing was a hard task. But what about school fees? Living in poverty without fees to pay for high school was catastrophic. I stayed at home the entire first term when my group had already joined their respective high schools. Totally desperate, I lost all my self-esteem and childhood dreams of going to university. There was no light. I felt that was the end of the road to my schooling.

Yet, right now I am at university as I share with you. Something must have happened. On 15th May 2011, my Head Teacher, Mr. Jeremiah Amulundu of Ebuchira Primary School, came to my home. He told me to call my parents because there was something he wanted to discuss with them. He informed my parents that he had heard a rumour that his best student had not attended school and it was already second term. My parents were frank and boldly told him that they could not raise the Ksh 70,000 to pay school fees at Kakamega High School, where I had been offered a chance. He was so touched that he took an initiative that changed my life. He introduced me to St. Patrick›s Ikonyero Secondary School, a two and half kilometre distance from my home.

The story continues. Mr. Amulundu paid with his own money Ksh.5000 as part of my school fees. He also informed the school principal, Mrs. Mukula, that I should remain in school at all costs as I was a promising, determined, hardworking and disciplined student. Our family sold everything that could be sold and that was just enough to purchase basic necessities, a pair of shoes and one shirt. I attended class with borrowed trousers. Life is what you make it!

Please do not feel pity for me. However, the reality is that I had nothing that was required for admission such as a mathematical set, an English dictionary, a Bible, a Kiswahili kamusi (dictionary) and all those necessary academic tools. By now half the second term was gone and I had lost a half a year of learning.

I settled down to serious study in the middle of second term. I was in a desperate situation as the academic system remained unchanged. I failed terribly on my first examination in high school, managing to score a C-. I was in position 93 out of 150 students. This was the first time I felt the pain of failing an examination. I felt like giving up, but something funny happened. My principal was impressed with my results! Achieving such a grade in one half of a term was worth her recommendation. I was encouraged despite the irony of being a champion in academics all my life.

Declining the August holiday, I remained in school throughout. I had to cover all I had missed. School fees were in arrears and that was all I thought about as I covered the five kilometres each day to attend school. Most of the time I was without food to eat.

I resumed my third term in Form One after the principal allowed me to improve academically. I woke at three o›clock in the morning to avoid being late. Was danger lurking in the darkness? I never thought of that in my life. Remember my home was located deep in the interior in the village and the school is in the vicinity of Kakamega town. Enduring the morning cold with no cardigan or pullover, I adapted to survive on the long journey. I collected the early morning dew from the napier grass along the side of the road. This was my source of fresh clean water to drink. God protected me without my knowledge from the dogs and other dangers on the road.

By the end of the school year I was the second-best student. Then it happened. I was awarded a CES Kenya/Canada scholarship. That is the greatest achievement in my life. CES has made me who I am today. I am very grateful and I owe CES my life. I maintained a brilliant record in school despite the small challenges like lack of food, walking long distances, dangers at night and many more I can't even remember or are not worth sharing.

To be lucky you must be honest and faithful. I won my teachers' affection and the principal used to give me some cash to use for things like soap and pens. With such special care and attention, I had no other option but to excel. I maintained discipline and determination which today I believe are the pillars of success.

I have come to believe that all great stories have a humble beginning. I am determined in my life to have a great story to share and to motivate and inspire others.

I completed Form Four, achieving the second highest grade in the school. I applied for a CES Leadership scholarship, one of eight of twenty-four that applied. I received a call from Mr. Khaemba and he told me that I had made it. I would be sponsored for my university education. In my family I am the first to get to university, so I was very happy. Now I am almost out of school. CES has been paying my fees for the past seven years, backing my education, my accommodation, upkeep, school fees, everything.

I secured a chance to study at the most prestigious university in Kenya, the University of Nairobi. As I reflect on my story, I once again thank CES Kenya/Canada for creating a Leadership scholarship for me. I am determined to produce exemplary results in my academic life and make a contribution to society.

At the University of Nairobi I have learned one thing. Management is the key to success in life. The environment is challenging and one must manage time, money, friendship and all that is worth being managed.

CES means so much to me. Thanks for your extended support. Be blessed abundantly. I thank the Almighty for CES and for its global initiative of supporting education.

Mzungu asks, "CES has given you a lot and has covered your university studies. What have you done to help yourself and others along the way?"

You see in Kenya, when you finish high school, there's that duration, almost one year, to stay at home before you join university. If you are government sponsored, there is a cutoff point in which the government pays part of your fees, you pay the rest. But some of us come from very humble backgrounds. We can't raise the money, so we have to get some funding.

When I was teaching as a CES Intern, I was absorbed in my own school, the one that I learned in. I encouraged the students as I was previously one of them, and I made it to university. But it's not for everyone, I told them. You have to be smart and work hard.

While I was working, I was being paid to support myself. I was not just staying at home for one year. That's a waste. In Kenya, you finish in November, but you do not join university until September of the following year. All that time, you are just at home. I taught school for nine months. They wrote me a very good letter of how I motivated the students; and, some of them are now going to university.

I'm still in university and I also have a small printing business. I started it when I was in first year, during my first long holiday. You see, we go on a holiday for four months. Our academic year lasts from September to April the following year. From there you are free until September, so there's a break of four months.

In Nairobi, I worked as a laboratory technician. I discovered that the printing and paper for the exams were substandard. I had received a computer from CES Kenya, and that's when I got the idea that besides doing the biochemistry work, I could do something more. I started printing exams. So that's something I do besides the biochemistry and school.

In Kenya, up to Class Eight (equivalent to a North American Grade Eight) education is free. Some people just finish Class Eight and they drop out of school. Some just reach Form Four (the end of high school), and that is the end of their education. So, getting into a university is a privilege. When I go to my village, I'm like an icon there. So if someone's advising people, they say, "Be like Viewtone." I'm motivating people.

The key to life is to give back and demonstrate that your goal on earth is to help others. By doing so and keeping others in your heart and mind, it is possible to be successful.

Melvin Wafula SICHUKA *BBM (Business Management),*
Moi University (2019)
CES Alumni Executive, Entrepreneur

Growing up in Namirama Village near Kakamega, I was the fourth born child in a family of six children. My mother did all she could; most importantly, providing for our education. My father, who worked some distance away in a tea plantation in Nandi County, abandoned us leaving the burden to my mother alone. She died when I was in Standard Six, aged twelve years. I never gave up on life; in fact, my mom's death made me stronger and more hardworking, and I always believed I was the one to redeem my family.

Achieving 356 marks in the KCPE, I was invited to attend Friends Namirama Girls SS. It also happened to be a school to which CES Canada was associated. Principal Mrs Granda Oprong' forwarded my case as a totally orphaned needy student and I was accepted, thank God. This one event changed my entire life.

The day I entered the CES program I had but one wish: to be successful in everything I did. In this way, I could become the light of my family and a role model to the entire society. Regardless of one's background, I believed it was possible to improve on a challenging situation.

Four years in Namirama Girls were not easy. I thank God, my teachers, my guardians and the entire CES team for not letting me give up. I told myself, "Girl, giving up is not an option. You must work hard. All eyes are on you." I never lacked sanitary towels, soap, and other basics because of CES. I was never sent home for lack of school fees. My only task was to study.

In 2014, I sat for my KCSE and fortunately scored an A-. I was the happiest girl in the world. My dream had come true. Since the school opened in the 70's, no student had ever scored that high. The record had been set!

Prior to entering university, CES gave me a chance to work as an intern Teacher Assistant in my school. As a role model, I helped others change their perspective on life. In the summer of 2015 – another miracle! I was accepted as one of the seven CES graduates for a university scholarship. I had just received an admission letter from Moi University to study in the Bachelor of Business Management (BBM) program. Beginning in September 2015, CES paid for my school fees and living expenses.

I was also enrolled in the CES School of Continuing Studies on-line leadership training program, graduating in October 2017. I am currently in my third year and second semester, proceeding to a co-op assignment in the area of finance and banking.

Recently I was elected as the secretary of the CES alumnus group. I am honoured and humbled to serve in this capacity. The group is giving back to society as we work together as alumni to help needy students. Just as CES 'bailed us out' of our bad situations, we do the same for others. We want to make them smile; it is a good feeling knowing that you made someone else happy.

I would like to extend my appreciation to the CES Canada President Mr. Michael Frederiksen, CES Kenya patron Mr. Malik Khaemba, Faculty Advisor Patricia Makori and the entire CES team. I would also like to thank donors from Canada for the financial support they've offered me all this while. I do not have enough words to thank you for making me who I am, and for making my dream come true. Despite the ups and downs you have stood by me, you never gave up on me and never found any reason to doubt my ability. I am very grateful to be part of the CES family. I love you so much. I owe the entire CES team my life, my career and my success.

I believe that kindness has the power to change the world. Because of your genuine and compassionate heart, you remind me that the world needs more kindness and caring people; you are my role model. Thank you! May God bless you abundantly with success in all you do to help so many.

Here's a quote I particularly like to share: "The measure of greatness in the society is found in the way it treats those in need, those who have nothing apart from their poverty" (Pope Francis).

Immeldah Khasoa KHAKUMA
CES Alumna and student at Egerton University

Being a part of CES KENYA/CANADA is an absolute miracle. I still find it hard to believe that I could ever study at the university level. Just like many others, I had a dream. Despite a poor and humble background and inability of my family to pay school fees, I never gave up hope. I achieved the KCPE in 2010 and was admitted to a district high school. Somehow, I completed Form One; however, I was not permitted to start Form Two because I had not paid my Form One school fees.

With the encouragement of my elder sister Sheilah, also a CES sponsored student, I began studying at home. At the end of the year I applied to write the exams. I passed! Even the teachers were shocked. I used to recite poems. As the school AGM was nearing, I prepared to present a poem written by my father. That was the day that everything changed.

A professor from Kenyatta University was invited to the AGM. He was touched by my dramatic presentation and later promised to pay my school fees for Forms 3 and 4. The head teacher used that money to clear the balance for the previous years. So again, I was stranded. In 2012 CES Kenya made a decision to add two students to each of their schools. Imagine how happy I was to be selected to receive a CES scholarship. I worked hard to achieve a B+ in the KCSE. As a result, I was invited to join the CES mentorship program as a teacher assistant at my school.

In 2015 I received a university scholarship (Egerton University Bachelor Agriculture Education) and the following year was invited to be part of the CES School of Continuing Education Leadership Training Program. I have learned much and I dearly appreciate the CES organization that has had such a great impact on my education.

To all those Canadian donors who have provided scholarships for me and others, I can say that your work is God given. I thank you for changing my life in such a positive way.

Enock OMBUNA
CES Graduate, Murang'a University of Technology

I was part of a large family, being the fourth born out of seven children. Despite the fact that my parents never completed their education, they went through struggles and hard experiences day and night to care for our education. All they earned came from the small piece of land we owned, approximately half an acre. We could spend days and nights on an empty stomach and were being frequently sent away from school for fees. I didn't give up but kept on working hard.

I finished my primary education, but because of the financial condition of my parents, they weren't able to pay for the educational needs of the whole family. Acquiring basic needs became difficult.

My father had to pay for my elder brother to attend college at that time, as well as pay the school fees for both of us. It soon became impossible. This forced my elder brother to go out and look for a job so that he could help us meet the needs. It is through this that my older brother and sister were able to attend school before the situation worsened again.

However, when it turned to me, things were not on my side. There wasn't money to afford the national school I was called to join. In addition, the local school could not afford me anymore. I had nothing to do other than just to stay home. One month later, after all schools had resumed, I took a step forward to seek advice from my friends who had completed their education. One of them advised me to go one by one to all local schools around and plead for mercy from individual principals.

I arrived at Namundera mixed secondary school and that was where I got mercy with conditions. It was a local school where I had never dreamed of studying. It was conditional that I would only be accepted to be enrolled if I passed the end term exam. I did my best and attained A plain. This really surprised and amazed the principal. He went on and suggested to the board of school management that I was one hardworking, needy student.

This is how I got into the CES sponsorship, and after that I was successful in all my final exams to Form 4. I was grateful and happy. I also received partial scholarships from CES to attend university. I am now pursuing Year 1 of a Bachelor of Education Science program at Murang›a University of Technology. I am glad and thank you for your support. Your guidance nurtures me to be a compassionate leader in the future. Currently, I am a class representative of all education science students in the first year of studies.

Mildred WASIKE

Student, University of Shanghai University for Science and Technology

My name is Mildred Wasike, I am the third born in a family of four. I grew up in the rural part of western Kenya, in Kakamega, Navakholo sub-county.

I attended primary school near my home and attained the high marks needed to attend a provincial secondary school. Coming from a poor background, my parents couldn't afford to raise the required school fees. They were small scale farmers, living on a half hectare of land, mostly growing bananas. But being Christians, we believed that God could make a way. I managed to join Sidikho SS which was close to my home. That made it possible for me to help my parents with farm work on weekends and house chores after school.

While in form two, my parents couldn't raise the required school fees in my second year. But since I was always the best in my class, Principal Mr. Issa Ramadhan never sent me home for school fees. Because he knew my background, he sympathized and introduced me to a certain NGO called CES Kenya, an organization comprised of volunteers both from Kenya and Canada. I learned that CES aimed at promoting and improving education and health for the less privileged in the rural western Kenya. I had heard they were building schools, libraries, hand wash stations, sources of clean water, dairy farms and other food supply sources. The best part was that CES also provided scholarships to students in secondary schools, with some sponsored to university level. I was granted a scholarship while in form two until I finished my secondary school education.

That was a dream come true in my life. By acquiring an education, I was sure of becoming a successful person in my life and society at large. I always had a passion for engineering. Being a determined and hardworking student, I completed my final exam in high school and did so well that I secured another scholarship from the county government to study abroad in China. I count myself very lucky because I was the only one from our county selected, and one of twenty across Kenya.

In China, I could pursue a degree in my dream course, biomedical engineering. I was so happy but at the same time afraid to go to that far off place away from home. It was my first time travelling anywhere. From that day I believed that no matter where one comes from, his or her dreams are always valid. My first days in China were tough— the weather, food, language, the people and the culture at large. With time I got used to it. I had to spend one year studying the Chinese language because my course is only offered in Chinese. It was quite challenging for me at first, especially the writing part of the characters. There are other Kenyans in China studying different courses and I have come to appreciate this small group that remind me of home.

At first I thought I would have to remain in China studying at the Shanghai Medical University of Technology until I completed the program. That would have meant five years being away from home and my family. But in 2018 I had an emergency where I had to upgrade my Kenyan passport. It could not be done in China. I had to return home within six months or my passport would run out and I would be stranded. Neither the Kenyan nor Chinese government made any provision for me to return home.

Being part of the CES family, I knew I could ask for support from them. All along they had been supporting me personally, spiritually and financially. In February 2019 I travelled back home to renew my passport. CES Canada paid for my ticket and I am so grateful, I never take such kindness for granted. I can't thank them enough. My special gratitude goes to Mr. Michael Frederiksen, who has always been checking on me every time, and who also organized a friend to visit me while I was in China. I am not forgetting all the CES friends and family who made it possible for me to make it home safely and attaining the passport on time. May the Almighty God bless you and your families abundantly.

Lastly, in my future I would like to create a foundation as a way of giving back to society. I am hoping to provide scholarships to the underprivileged girls in my community. Then I would like remind everyone that all things are possible. Stay focused, work hard, stay humble and above all, trust God.

Edwin Juma Edwin NYONGESA *BA Education, Maseno University (2016)*
Chairman, CES Kenya Alumni

I look back and truly thank God for getting this far. I am a young man born out of wedlock, where my father rejected me at a very tender age and my mom chose to raise me on her own. I remember at the age of three years, she left me with my grandparents and got married to another man. He unfortunately passed on, leaving her with four children whom she struggled to raise. From the moment she left me, I have lived without truly knowing what it means to have parental care and love.

I think all these challenges are what has propelled me to work hard and keep on going as far as I have. CES rescued me in 2010 when I was in my third form in Shieywe Secondary School in Kakamega. Were it not for CES, it is possible that my academics would have suffocated at that stage and I never would have made it to university. That is totally true, beyond a reasonable doubt. When it dawned on me that I was now sponsored, it felt like a breath of fresh air within myself. Nothing could stop me from working hard. There was a renewed focus in me that even my teachers couldn't believe.

What CES is doing is actually touching and transforming the lives of young people. It has changed me and for sure it will affect my family and community as well. I am truly proud of you (CES) and keep praying for the good work you are doing. I feel I have been born again.

Currently I am working on a Masters of Education in Kiswahili. But when I first graduated from Maseno University in the year 2016, it was with a Bachelors of Education in Kiswahili and History. Presently I have decided to major in Kiswahili as a language, although history still remains a strong interest.

I went to Shieywe Secondary School where I came to meet CES when in Form 3. It was a tough time for me. I was finishing my third year at the Secondary level, and wanted to do my final year, but I had no school fees. CES then came into the picture.

From the start of my education at the high school level, I was being sponsored by my uncle. But this was not enough and so we kept struggling. If you don't have money and if you are not stable enough in your mind, you will end up depressed. You will lose hope in life, you will think that life doesn't make sense because you are expected to be in school. Without funds you are sent home to get that cash. You go home, find there's no money, and are forced to stay there. And then? While you stay stranded at home, your colleagues are learning, so there is no way you will catch up with those in your class.

If you stay home, there are some repercussions. You lose the content that was taught when you were not there. That means, even if you catch up with the others, you take a lot of time to reach their level again. And even if you catch up with them, you will not really be at the level you could have been. That means your academics or performance will be drastically affected.

But when a support comes into the picture like it came to me, it is like a renewal of something. You know when a snake is getting older, it must renew its skin or scales. That is what happened to me. I felt a new surge, a new inspiration, a new hope that was coming in. That is how I grabbed the opportunity with all my hands and said this is it! No excuse! You have to give it your best.

Until then I was not performing that well. I was trying, but I could be number five or seven out of a possible of 150 students. But then with the CES support that came into the picture, my performance shot up. I now began playing between number one, two or three. Until I finished my secondary education, I continued to perform well.

Here's what it's like to have your fees paid. You feel settled, you feel there's someone who cares for you and it has come at the right time. If your school fees are paid, it means you only need to wake up early in the morning, go to school, study, read hard, come back home in the evening, continue with your studies, no interruption.

It remains now your responsibility alone to get settled down. And, another inspirational aspect is you've been given a chance, and you can only reciprocate by giving your best. Maybe, this doesn't mean giving money, but rather doing what you are supposed to do in your studies. So you grab that opportunity. It inspires you. It changes everything within you, and you have to give it your best. And I think for my case it was a game changer in my mind and even in my life.

Let me share an experience I had with two former colleagues, friends of mine at the time. At one point they had some support for school fees. But they didn't concentrate on their studies and after we did our final examination, they didn't perform very well. But if you had an opportunity to meet them you would see the difference. Initially we were a group of three people. But then out of the three I made it, but the other two didn't. How is that? Am I just lucky or favoured? Not really. The value of hard work and total focus cannot be underestimated.

My life now is very different from theirs. One of them is at Eldoret. I'm told he sells used clothing, or as we call it, '*mitumba*'. And the other one is at Kisumu. I'm not really sure what he does. From the time I've known him he still struggles. So they have to use other means to make a living. But for my case, you see I've gone to university, finished, and now doing my second degree. What a difference. But I take nothing for granted, for without others in my life I would not have succeeded.

Mzungu asks, "CES provides moral support and encouragement as well as paying fees. How does this help?"

Yes, moral support for sure. I remember at one point there were some ladies from CES Canada that came to visit us at school. These w*azungu (plural form of mzungu in Kiswahili)* came with a bag full of mosquito nets for the students and some other items. This really made an impact. For someone who has never seen such kind of a bag, someone who has never slept under such a mosquito net, it really helps. So it's kind of playing something psychologically in you, telling you, "This is it. You've got it. Your very own net! You will be spared from the dreaded malaria. Somebody cared enough to relieve you from your suffering." We were encouraged and our spirits lifted.

Besides that, we have very many young people supported by the CES program. They don't have any moral support. No one cares if they make it or not. So when you (CES) meet them you inspire them, you challenge them, you say, "We are here to support you, we are here to be with you through this journey and you're going to make it."

It changes their game, it changes their perception about life that even if they don't get it from their family setup, there is a family somewhere and this is CES! This family loves them. This family is concerned about them and is looking after them to make sure they are comfortable in all that they do.

Just to explain: By the time we were finishing our secondary education, CES was just sponsoring to that level. So when I joined the university for my first degree, the support was not there. But out of that I managed to get a government loan. That helped to see me through to my second degree.

Only when you finish university, there is a burden on your shoulder because the loan accumulated is close to around 200,000 Kenyan Shillings (*mzungu checked the currency exchange rate online and that's about CDN$2,700*). So now after you finish, when you get a job, you need to pay back that loan.

I am trained to be a teacher. My vision is that, given an opportunity, I will be teaching. And maybe my teaching will begin in a high school. But as young as I am, I have already begun to expand my scope. When I'm done with my master's studies, I can expand it to the college or university level, But my starting point before I get to the higher levels is high school level.

Last year I volunteered to teach for one full year at one of the CES schools. This year I am focusing on my master's. But hopefully by next year God willing, I may get an employment with the government, beginning from the high school level. But then from there I can expand my scope of maybe teaching in a college level, and maybe in university.

What I've come to appreciate is that you cannot just fix your mind in one direction and you have it stuck there. I am open to new perspectives, new ways of thinking. I have a rich understanding and facility in the Kiswahili language, I can do an editorial job in a newspaper or in a communication centre.

Life in its fullness has taught me humility the hard way. I grew up and missed out on much love I most needed from my own father. I have never come to know his whereabouts, but He who is our father in heaven taught me how first to love other people. l now I understand how to love myself. I have given myself to Him above, to His Word and to finally investing in myself and positioning my life for the higher calling and servant life of humanity. This is the beauty of learning to trust in God. As much as has been given to me, so I pray I will give much more to this world in my lifetime. I am not what I was, and I will not be what I am, but what I do know is that what I am today is because of CES.

When I think of my colleagues, the CES Alumnus who now number over 700, I know they will in time become like a team of nation builders and help Kenya to grow and prosper. May we take our good time to learn from each other, network, enrich, equip and build each other up. Who knows? Maybe the one to lift you up is just near you in this great team. I tell young CES graduates, "Feel inspired and energized to face your tomorrow because it is just budding and about to flower. Let the full process take its course. You shall get there. Do not rush it. Do not force it through. It will break for you."

Mzungu says: Your poetry and way of expressing yourself shows a special talent and gift. What messages do you want to pass on to your generation?

"We can always ensure we make the best out of our environment, especially from those people who surround us. Regardless of the challenges, be the person who moulds pots from clay soil, as dirty as it seems to be. Never ever give up on anyone. Never ever despise anyone. Never ever run away from your failures. At least there's always that chance to remould yourself and life."

"Master the art and skill of reaching out to your fellows and never die in silence. A single word spoken could be your lifetime saviour. Who knows the person who could be listening to you at that time."

"Have a vision. Find your purpose in life. Follow your dream but break it into manageable sets. Take small steps to get there."

"Sometimes you are unsatisfied with your life, while many people in this world are dreaming of living your life. A child on a farm sees a plane fly overhead and dreams of flying. But, a pilot on the plane sees the farmhouse and dreams of returning home. That's life!! Enjoy yours."

Mzungu asks, "Edwin, you are now heading up the CES Alumni Group. Tell us a little about what you hope to accomplish as a team of CES grads."

After CES began the sponsorship some years ago, it reached a point, that those who were sponsored asked themselves, "What is the best way we can give back as a lesson learned from what has been done for us?"

So a small group of people came together in the year 2014 and they sat in a restaurant here at the Sheywe Conference Centre. Out of it they adopted the strategy of coming together and pulling together as a way of giving back to the society. An executive team was created to oversee how the alumni chapter could open up and begin running. We began the CES Alumni as a small group of twenty.

I happened to be among the leaders in the first executive committee, serving as the vice secretary. We wrote the constitution for the alumni and were successful in founding a CBO (Community Based Organization). Some followup activities included organizing the jiggers campaign, helping over 500 children in five primary schools. We were also involved in coordinating the annual Canada Day Run (since 2011) at Masinde Muliro University of Science and Technology.

Mzungu asks, "What are jiggers?"

Jiggers (also spelled *chiggers*) are mites that enter into your toe or into your finger. These are defined as a tiny mite whose parasitic larvae live on or under the skin of warm-blooded animals, where they cause irritation and dermatitis and sometimes transmit scrub typhus. They begin eating up from inside, itching and then the area where they have infested, begins to form what we call a wound. The wound swells and it spreads across the flesh. So you find it could end up eating all your fingers and they become so painful.

For the young ones, if the toes have been affected they cannot wear shoes, they cannot walk comfortably. Because it is itching, it is painful. It is impossible for the children to stay in school to learn comfortably. So most of them even, if they go to school, will focus on the jiggers and not concentrate on learning. To overcome that one, we organized campaigns where we sensitized society as a measure to overcome it. They need to maintain the highest possible level of cleanliness. Again for the children, they need shoes to overcome (and prevent) that problem.

When you sensitize them about this and teach them how they can overcome it, the situation improves. We went back the following year and found an improved story with those same children. At least the jigger infestation was reduced and children could go to school comfortably in a pair of shoes that CES had given them. That was our first project as alumni.

Second, we've also been engaged and involved in doing hand washing activities. We need to appreciate that washing hands with soap is very important as matters of health are concerned. But for children and for most people they do not know the importance of hand-washing with soap. I remember it was in our news report that a high percentage of people will go to the toilet and never wash their hands at all. And you understand, this is what brings on diarrhea and many other health issues. But we have gone ahead with hand washing activities, training young people to embrace that as an idea to maintain good health in their lives.

Again we also did work providing eyeglasses to people at the Ingotse Medical Clinic where one of us works. CES graduate Busuku Musli Wetende is the chief medical officer who helped organize the event.

Then towards last year December, we elected a new group of leaders to take over the leadership and to see what else we could do. And it is out of that meeting, I was elected as the chairman of that group. Melvin Wafula is the secretary, Allan Utumbi is the assistant secretary, Mwanarabu Otswang is the treasurer, and then we have the vice-chairman Dennis Were. So we now form the executive committee of five people.

From that, we have come up with a different strategy and formulated a new vision for the alumni. We have a long term focus in life as a way of giving back to the society. We believe it is possible since most of us are now graduating from universities and within a short time will be getting a job. We should be putting our resources together and we can begin initially by at least sponsoring two students. We are beginning that way, so that maybe in the future we grow slowly, slowly.

We walk with two students right from Form 2 level. CES came into my life at Form 3. But if we start at the Form 2 level, it will make a big difference. We pay for school fees when a student is about age fourteen of high school. So we support them until they finish their high school studies. I am just seeing us complimenting what CES has been doing for us.

We have also made a commitment to the Divine Providence Orphanage in Kakamega. This Christmas we will visit and bring gifts, play games, have some fun and eat a meal together. We also provide new clothing and bring food and sacks of rice, maize and beans for the sisters at the orphanage. By showing them some love we too will feel the same coming back to us. Several alumni remember Canadian Sharyn Poole and her love for these orphaned children. Each time they return they honour her and it is also a way to give back. The Alumni have been there now three times and we wish to continue these visits.

The CES Alumni regularly visit schools to provide motivational speeches and talk to students. We have mentored our students in personal hygiene and health through discussions and demonstrations of hand washing with soap. Recently the CES Alumni executive took part in coordinating and presenting at the Form 4 Leadership Training Conference that focused on topics such as: Dealing with Peer Pressure, Career and Life skills and Preparing for College and University.

So there are many ways we as CES Alumni can give back to society. Alumni are coming together. Like family we are continuing with the association, building relationships, networking, and developing leaders. We had a first set of leaders that had a vision. They have graduated and moved to the next level in society. We are the second ones, and we will be moving to the next levels as well. We will have a third one, again shaping leaders in society by giving them the opportunity to do whatever they can do to improve the lives of others.

Graduates of the CES program have built their own community spirit by volunteering and creating education scholarships for needy youth. Members of the Executive are, left to right: Elicah Mayukuva, Dennis Were, Mwanarabu Otswang, Melvin Wafula and Chairman Edwin Nyongesa

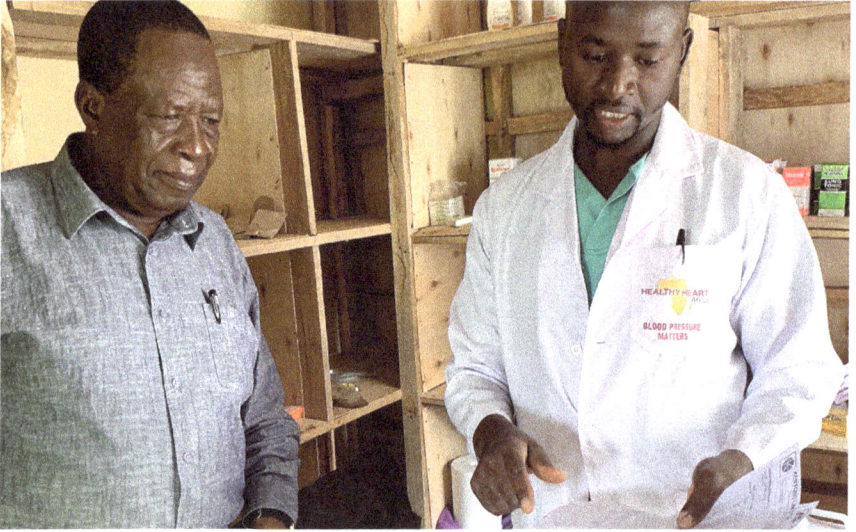

CES Patron and co-founder Malik Khaemba (left) meets with CES graduate and medical doctor Busuku Musili (right) at the clinic he founded. The Ikhavi Medical Centre serves over 10,000 people in Bushiri-Uzima villages and is open 24/7 each day of the year.

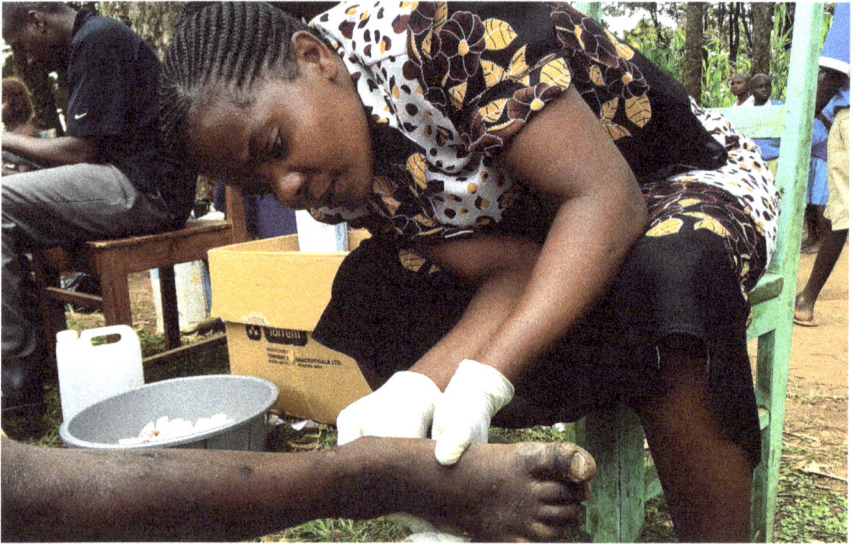

Many CES graduates have achieved impressive careers that help their community. Among them is CES Grad Metrine Mayende, Community Health Nurse. Here she volunteers her time for elementary school students suffering from jiggers. CES Alumni have coordinated three jiggers medical outreach events treating over 1200 children and youth.

CES Grads Mourine Muchanji (left), Immeldah Khasoa and Linda Wabwire (right) attend the Tropical Medicine and Eye Clinic in Kakamega. Mourine's albinism left her with disabilities, including limited vision and hearing. Here two friends Immeldah and Linda help Mourine to obtain the eyeglasses she needed to succeed in her learning.

The first CES online leadership study group were selected for their academic achievements, community volunteerism and potential for leadership. Here enjoying their 2017 graduation ceremonies are left to right: Melvin Wafula, Allan Utumbi, Milridah Ominde, Immeldah Khasoa, CESCED Principal Patricial Makori, Sharon Walekhwa, Dennis Were and Viewtone Achaga.

CES Kenya Office Manager Sarah Nabongo (left) and Patricia Makori (right), Principal of the CES School of Continuing Education (CESCED) relaxing at the Rondo Retreat Centre. Respected and beloved as "big sisters" to CES students, they offer guidance in career and education planning to navigate the challenges of growing up.

Part V

Towards Social Justice

CHAPTER 17:
Wisdom from the Front Lines

"If we respect each other, we can always love each other"

Kenyan proverb

Mzungu says: CES is a small organization that keeps costs to a minimum. One of the things I like most about CES is that it hasn't tried to tele-operate this thing from Canada. Right from the start, the driving force and decisions came from people close to the front lines, in Kenya. Most of these have given their time on a volunteer basis. We have also been blessed with the support of two people who have helped the organization's work in the office and in the field. These writings are from Patricia Makori and Sarah Nabongo. Patricia talks of the practical issues facing girls seeking an education; Sarah talks of her role as a "big sister" and part-time office support for CES Kenya.

LET'S MAKE MENSTRUATION MAINSTREAM

by Patricia Makori, CES Kenya Director
Principal, CES School of Continuing Education (CESCED)

Since 2007 CES Canada has been providing our girls with feminine hygiene health products and education on healthy living. The PAD initiative has created quite a stir in rural western Kenya. The girls are talking about it and all reports indicate that their attendance in secondary school has improved, and they are much more knowledgeable about their menstrual cycle and the physical changes occurring as they mature.

CES Canada provides the funding and its partner CES Kenya delivers the resources and education. CES representatives, as well as Canadian volunteers, meet with CES scholarship students to share their learning experiences and discuss topics like healthy living, sex and dealing with their monthly period.

Although things are slowly changing in Kenya, there remains a huge need for girls to become aware of the issues surrounding their sexuality. Take for example Alice Sunguti. When she got her first period she cried, afraid that she was dying. Embarrassed and terrified, she stuffed bits of an old blanket inside herself to try and stem the bleeding. Too frightened to tell her parents what was happening, she kept quiet. She spent her school day glued to her desk, terrified blood would leak out, exposing her to ridicule from her classmates.

Today she is no longer afraid. Alice is now 17 years of age, and she is part of the CES PAD program. "Menstruation is a normal developmental process that happens to all girls and I am no longer embarrassed. I can't wait to give lessons to some girls and reassure them that none of my teachers, friends, desk mates and parents will know I have my menstruation."

We know there is a problem when as many as five out of ten girls in rural Kenya are missing school during menstruation. It is high time that girls have access to the sanitary products they need and receive reproductive rights education without shame or secrecy.

According to information from FSG Menstrual Health Landscape, 65% of Kenyan girls are unable to afford sanitary pads. For most families living in acute poverty, the need for people to buy food is more important than purchasing sanitary pads for a girl. Girls resort to using rags and mattress stuffing, causing infections and painful sores. The situation is so bad that girls feel they need to have sex as a way to get the money to buy the pads.

Products alone are not the solution. The other essential element is to have a basic understanding of reproductive health and what is happening physically. It is also important for schools to assist girls by providing separate bathrooms for girls with doors and locks for privacy. In rural areas of Kenya, only a third of schools have made this possible. Many teachers are also uncomfortable talking about or teaching menstruation. Without the PAD project, many of our CES sponsored girls would have no opportunity to talk to a family member. Being orphaned they tend to get faulty information from their friends.

There is a need in Kenyan schools to teach girls about reproductive health. Curriculum in both primary and secondary classes is essential. Teachers need to be empathetic and trained to teach what many would say are sensitive topics. Access to sanitary pads should be a right, not a privilege for the few that can pay for it.

Let's talk about it and find real solutions. Let's break the taboo where we don't discuss these subjects. Let's engage girls in a learning process that helps them to be informed, knowledgeable, and able to establish their own identity and purpose in life. Let's make menstruation mainstream.

MENTORING AND EMPOWERING YOUTH

by Sarah Nabongo, Executive Office Coordinator CES Kenya

Mzungu says: Sarah is the key staff person in the office at CES Kenya. She also works with KEEF (Kenya Education Endowment Fund) and is currently studying Business Administration at Kenyatta University. She is the first point of contact that CES has with students – helping them through their issues, problems and victories. From my conversations with students and teachers, Sarah is a "big sister" to many of the students, particularly the girls, helping them navigate the difficult issues of adolescence.

I have had the pleasure of working with CES Canada and CES Kenya for the past six years. During this time I have welcomed hundreds of students, parents and school personnel to the office. Each person is important to me; each has a story and a plea for support of some kind. One thing CES has taught me is that all people can do something to better their lot in life. When CES considers support for a student, the question is always asked, "What can you do to support yourself?" When students are accountable and they make their own contribution, they will appreciate more the scholarship that CES can offer them.

The government pays some of the fees for the students, yet there is still part of the fee that the parent is supposed to pay. For example, the lunch program fee, textbooks and other costs for field trips are mandatory. We find that some of the families can't afford to pay the lunch program and provide textbooks and uniforms for their kids, even with the government chipping in to help. That's how CES comes in, to support such families. This is a really great help because as we can see in the testimonies here, without CES coming into these students' lives, some would not have been what they are today.

I have had a chance to interact with students seeking support through a secondary scholarship. This has been accomplished through school visitations every year. I meet these students one on one, talk to them and find out how they are faring. During these sessions I also mentor, encourage, and give studying tips, as well as being there as the person they look up to.

Kenyan students tend to confuse 'fear' and 'respect'. In my interaction with students, I have learned that they fear facing their teachers, parents or guardians. When talking to them I normally encourage them to respect their teacher and not to fear them.

Most of the students are not confident enough to face their teachers and explain to them what they want. However, through my talks with them, they realize that what they have been doing is not right. This encourages them and also makes them improve in their studies. They can have confidence when consulting their teachers to get help in the subjects they don't understand.

Girls may fear informing their parents and teachers that maybe they don't have sanitary towels. Students see me as person they can easily relate to.

The transition towards supporting university students is a great idea. We find that lack of funds makes students not complete their university studies within the stipulated period, as most of them are forced to defer their studies in order to look for funds.

Now that CES is shifting in that direction, this will enable these students to complete their studies on time. They can then get work and help their families, themselves, and decide to give back to the society through the CES Alumni.

Unemployment for young people is a huge problem in Kenya. As long as organizations like CES and other Canadian charities like KEEF and ACCES continue their work in Kenya, there is hope that many will be successful in their life and career. We cannot help everyone, for the resources are limited. For those we assist, there is always an expectation that they give a little towards helping the alumni create scholarships for needy students. In addition, they have to prove they can find funds elsewhere and have a budget that is acceptable to CES. That way they take ownership and not just a hand out.

Among the most enjoyable parts of my job is to put together health and hygiene kits for all our secondary students and deliver them personally at the school. For girls to receive hand cream lotion and the boys a bar of soap and toothpaste makes everyone so happy. For most of our students these are luxuries they otherwise could not afford. To be able to work with CES is a privilege. I enjoy mentoring our students. Every day is a challenge I accept, because I know there are friends in Canada to support me and the work we do at CES Kenya.

CHAPTER 18:

When Love Breaks Through

"Where there is a will, there is a way"

Kenyan Proverb

Address by Michael Frederiksen for the 15th Anniversary of CES Canada: August 23, 2018 at Masinde Muliro University of Science and Technology, Kakamega Kenya

After a 35 year career in teaching at the primary, secondary and post-secondary levels of education I had the extraordinary opportunity in 2004 to visit Kenya for three months. I taught at Garissa Boys HS in North East Province. At the same time, I was conducting research into the effects of the HIV/AIDS pandemic on the Kenya school system. That involved interactions with educators at the UNHCR camp at Dadaab, Kaimosi Teacher's College, Kenya Teachers Service Commission, Ministry of Education and thirty-three primary and secondary schools in Kenya. The plight of orphaned children and the desperate attempts of educators to meet the challenges of teaching were realities that deeply affected me. I returned to Canada with an intense desire to help alleviate the acute poverty I had seen. The tragic devastation of entire communities and the reality of an estimated 1.2 million youth unable to attend school due to lack of fees was unacceptable. The story of CES started with a few friends, twelve schools and twenty-four students. What has happened since then is nothing short of a miracle.

In 2019, CES Canada partners with CES Kenya and a family of twenty-five secondary schools. Since 2004 we have offered 2,500 education scholarships, created nine wells, and built classrooms, science and computer labs, dormitories, a kitchen facility and a new secondary school at Musaga, Navakholo sub-County. Projects to enhance student health and learning include the feminine hygiene PAD, 'hot meal' nutrition and de-worming initiatives. This year CES partners with Water Mission in Kenya to create a source of safe, clean water for three schools and a village of 4,000 people. The anticipated official opening is scheduled for August 2019.

In 2015 the CES School of Continuing Education was created. Pre-university Internships for our highest achievers provide two semesters of peer counselling and training as Teaching Assistants. The CES on-line Leadership Training program is providing skills in problem solving and effective communications for those in higher learning studies.

One of our graduates has received a full scholarship to study at the Shanghai School of Medical Technology in China. Graduates of the CES secondary school education program are attending college and university, emerging as teachers, research technologists, doctors, nurses, agriculturalists, farmers and auto mechanics. Many will make a strong contribution to their communities. All will have been given hope for a better day. The alternative of living in desperate circumstances, plagued by poverty, sickness, unemployment, early marriage, and early death is unacceptable.

A decade ago I did not consider myself to be a "humanitarian." I still don't. I am primarily an educator who believes in equal opportunity for all children to learn regardless of their race, culture or geographic location.

Each time I return to the field there is a renewed sense of urgency. Far too many bright students, hungry and thirsty for knowledge, are left to struggle on their own. School is not an option, and for some the daily needs of shelter, food and clothing are not adequately met. It breaks my heart to see students standing outside the school gate looking in. They deserve a chance to sit at the table of learning.

Life in Kenya is not easy. Sometimes the weather is hot, the water limited and electrical power is cut off. People suffer and there are few luxuries. Roads are tough to navigate and things generally move at a slow pace. Dealing with bureaucracy and elements of corruption at all levels is stressful. It is too easy to fall into the, 'if these people don't care then why should I' way of thinking.

So why carry on business? A good question that demands a response. "Do you think you're making a difference?" I am asked. "Do you think it does any good?" And the more cynical ask, "Why bother?" or "Why not spend your time helping people here (in Canada) who need it more?" There is no simple answer.

Yet I return, time and again. I love Kenya. I love the people and I truly believe in the power of CES Canada to make a difference. Memories of fatigue wear off, the frustration abates, and within days I am inspired by the friendship, hospitality and fresh opportunities to create new hope.

Each of us has the capacity to contribute a small amount to the world while on planet Earth. We are put in this world for a reason – to care for the environment and the people in it. Our work in Kenya brings perspective to our lives in Canada. As we share their story with others it gives meaning to our own. When our passion inspires someone to help bridge the health and education gap between Canada and Kenya, that is good. If it helps others to engage in humanitarian activity, that is even better.

That's what makes CES so special. It's the people, the over 70 volunteers who have travelled to Kenya, donors that sacrifice to give, board members and many others who give time and resources to encourage our students. It's a community of friends in Thunder Bay who have built the St Agnes Dorm at Shikoti Girls HS and a brand new Musaga SS. It is individuals who decide to support an entire group of students at one of our twenty-five schools. It is people who care enough to donate to CES on a monthly basis. That's what keeps us going, that's what motivates. It's that unique joy that comes from working together for a great cause. It's those here in Kenya who fifteen years ago, had a vision to build a stronger, safer, better community and to give back some of the blessings they had received in life. The CES Kenya Board members, CES Principals, teachers, Board of

Managers and community members, parents, friends here at MMUST and a host of Kenyans, all volunteers have given what was never expected.

See now before you the amazing results, and be assured that what has been started will live long after we all retire from active community service. The blessings will continue to flow through the lives of those we have influenced and touched.

Does saving one child from poverty or one girl from an early marriage that often includes dying in childbirth make a difference? It does to them. And is doing nothing because one can accomplish little, a valid excuse to actually do nothing? Absolutely not. We cannot know the impact of our seemingly small actions. A child who doesn't die of malaria or Aids will perhaps be afforded the chance to attend school, become a teacher and contribute to his community. An educated student is in a far better position to provide for his or her family. A girl given an opportunity to go to school will do everything possible to ensure that happens for the next generation.

Too optimistic? Probably – but here is one simple response to those who ask the question "why?" It's what Mother Teresa would say, "We cannot all do great things, but we can all do small things with great love." We are indeed our brother's keeper. And since we are a global community, we are no longer isolated. We have a responsibility to help. Together we work to build a better future for Kenya's youth.

Let us consider and rejoice that 750 young people have graduated from the CES program. Some of these fine young men and women are here with us today at MMUST. Confidant and mature, these CES Alumni have come a long way. As agents of change, they now give back, multiplying the gift they have received. That's the reason CES Canada exists – to transform an unacceptable reality.

When Love Breaks Through

I went with nothing but a few Kenyan shillings
in search of something yet to be sealed
with only a smile and willing hands
and hope for the Kingdom revealed

nothing in this world could ever prepare
for the stories written on poverty's scroll
in a place where the taste of bitter-sweet fruit
explodes on the palate of the soul.

when love breaks through unexpected
like a tsunami it strikes full force
overwhelmed I rage at the demons
of injustice that feel no remorse

the little one at Providence Orphanage
holds out his hand to be held
love breaks through
at Bishop Sulumeti she reminds me
I must persevere when I feel faint
love breaks through
young girl walks in the darkness to Ikonyero
her dream to live and learn so alive
love breaks through
young man refuses to trade his Eshitari tie
for a brand new CES sports cap
love breaks through
blind boy at Thika
sees his way to freedom
love breaks through

orphans at Ngara Girls
shyly wave as we leave
love breaks through
Ibinzo girl in green and white
takes tops honours
love breaks through

out of Bukhakunga comes a doctor
Namundera's finest now a nurse
Makhukuni grad a proud teacher
Navakholo's finest an ICT instructor
love breaks through

When love breaks through there is hope
when love breaks through the burden is lighter
when love breaks through there is freedom
when love breaks life shines brighter

When love breaks through
the tyranny of injustice is brought to its knees
oh for a thousand moments like these

When love breaks through

Under the Acacia Tree Anthology
07/2012

CHAPTER 19:
Future of CES in Kenya

"Find shelter under a berry-bearing tree, not under one without"

Kenyan proverb

Interview with Malik Khaemba
September 2018 at Kakamega, Kenya

Community Education Services has two branches, CES Kenya and CES Canada. CES Canada's role is to do the funding for, and create awareness of our needs in Kenya. In the recent past, they have partnered with a foundation that has been providing funds particularly for university students. Besides our main aim to provide secondary and post secondary scholarships, we also carry out some other activities and infrastructure projects.

CES Kenya is the agent for CES Canada, and is responsible for carrying out work 'on the ground'. Since 2006 we have also done a few development programs. This includes water boreholes, as well as infrastructure at schools including Musaga SS, where CES Canada has provided eight classrooms and a kitchen facility. CES Canada sent the funds and CES Kenya made sure the money went into the construction of the school.

CES Kenya drilled boreholes at eight schools and created three hygiene hand wash stations so students now have clean, safe water. We have also provided a dairy operation at two schools. One is at St Mary Goretti

Shikoti School where we bought two cows. The other is at Bishop Sulumeti School, where we bought, through the support of the World Bank and the East Africa Agriculture Productivity Program, two dairy animals for the school, a vegetable and a zero grazing garden.

CES has played a role in the economic development of our schools. We built a complete dormitory at St Mary Gorreti Shikoti, which houses over 100 students. A group from Thunder Bay, Ontario came and put up that building with funds donated by CES Canada. At Eshitari SS, we constructed a well, a dining hall and adjoining kitchen. So we have carried out infrastructure development and we're extremely proud of that. We appreciate the efforts that CES Canada has put into improving the lives of the youth in our community schools.

We do not select the students; that is done by the Principals of the schools. But we do a vigorous follow-up process with all our schools and students at the beginning of the year, and after the selection has been done. This is to ensure that schools have given us the correct number and the right calibre of students. We also follow up on their performance from the previous year and provide encouragement to do even better the next year.

CES Canada felt that students in the program should be provided with insecticide-treated mosquito nets and personal hygiene health kits. Fewer students have been ill and classroom attendance has improved. While it is good to sponsor students and pay fees, some are still living under very unhygienic conditions. As we visit our schools, we have been giving each student a health kit and a treated anti-malaria mosquito net so that they can sleep under its cover.

CES Canada also came up with the idea of providing sanitary towels for the girls. When we visit schools, we supply pads for the girls, supported by counselling and education. This has been a very useful program because the Kenyan government has not developed a clear policy on this matter. They have attempted, but so far they have not come up with a program to ensure that the girl child is provided with sanitary towels.

Originally the pads were sent directly from Canada, but in subsequent years we have been given funds to purchase them locally. This helps the local economy. In January, when the funds come in and the school year is just starting, our CES Executive Office Manager, Sarah Nabongo purchases the supplies. Then when we visit the schools in February-March we issue those pads and nets to the students.

Overall, we see the positive results in the lives of the students we sponsor. We see them excel in their studies, and that matters particularly when they explain how they live at home. Most of the students we have supported come from poor families, and many have proceeded to university. A number of them have completed their studies, and are already in the labour market. We have someone who is now in charge of a mission hospital. Several who did medical training are already working in clinics.

After students have completed Form Four and have done their exams and met at least the minimum requirements to go to university, we continue to walk with them. To support a student in a private university is very expensive, so our decision to support only students at public universities is realistic. We have agreed as a matter of policy, that since the government pays some of the cost, CES could take on the rest of the fees.

In 2014, CES Canada committed to provide full scholarships to seven students, so that they receive their entire amount of fees, plus some money for upkeep. There are other students we take care of under a partial scholarship program in which CES pays some, based on the student's need and the availability of funds.

Here are the reasons why CES is changing its focus towards university students. We encourage students between Form One and Form Four to work hard. Those who listened have done so, have passed and gone on to higher studies. We have been doing this over a number of years and now we realize that the money to pay for university is enormous. We want to help them to succeed, so we asked ourselves, "Are we being unfair to stop support after Form Four?"

We think it is a good idea to now reduce the resources for high school students and transfer it to university students. When they have achieved well and wish to go further, we don't want to say we are unable to support them. These are the students who made sure that they moved from one level to the next level in secondary school, and we cannot afford to abandon them. We have also told the principals of the schools we have worked with, saying that CES is moving away from supporting high school students, and more towards helping University and middle college students. This is because resources are finite and we can't meet both needs any longer.

Mzungu asks, "Does this mean cutting off opportunities for high school students?"

That is a good observation; I would say that is true. You can complete Form Four, but you have not been trained in any profession. You just have an academic certificate, which cannot give you anything in terms of employment. You may be employed, maybe you can get a job at the government or a private office, but our focus is to ensure that these young people have a real chance of getting into a professional field by attending university. CES Canada has planned in collaboration with CES Kenya that by 2020, secondary students who are accepted by a university will be able to receive some level of funding.

CES Canada has connected with a foundation that supports two groups of students: Firstly, those who are on what we call full scholarship, for whom we pay the full fees and we also give them one computer each. The first group of eight has completed their Leadership Studies and will be graduating from University in 2019.

The six students who are just starting in 2018 will also receive computers for their Leadership studies and University work. These computers have come out of the ICT program which has just ended. We are going to ensure that each student gets one computer for their work. As well as paying all fees for the full scholarship students, we also give them money for their upkeep, for room and food. We don't expect that all the students we support should get a pass to University. Most teachers would agree that would be unrealistic.

One of our other programs is Information Computer Technology (ICT). We have engaged a group of teachers to provide computer information to the students that we support in our schools. This mobile computer lab project has been going on for the last three years, ending in 2018. It has been a very important program because by the time they have completed Form Four, the CES sponsored students are computer literate.

Then another key program is what we call our Internship program. It involves students who have passed with very high marks. Students who get a B+ and above are sent back into the high schools they attended. They act as interns while teaching and doing other support work. One reason we do this is to show that we appreciate that they have worked so hard to get the highest grades. Another reason for the program is that it gives them a chance to mentor the other students who think, "If this one made it, then I also can make it." Intern students like it because we pay them for six months or so, as they wait for their university studies to start. So those who are diligent, will have saved some money by the time they start university.

Another program we offer focuses on developing leaders. Community Education Services School of Continuing Education (CESCED) provides our full scholarship university students with on-line training. Principal Patricia Makori runs the whole program online, including all training and communications. Patricia teaches them mainly about leadership and entrepreneurial skills within a framework of community service.

We believe it is important to encourage our former students, the alumni, to join in our work. We have encouraged them to come up with a leadership team which consists of a chairman, secretary and treasurer. The main idea is that those who complete school, even if they're not joining university or college, should become members of this alumni group. Our main intention was to get students in a position to manage CES when we are not there. Now, we realize that many students finishing university need to look around for a job. Because we (the founders) have already aged and very soon we are going to phase out, we need to get one or two or three people who can succeed us and manage CES when we are not there. But over and above all that, we want to bring them together as alumni of CES. The alumni group has agreed to support one or two students. This is a team that has come together because they have been supported by CES Kenya, and now wish to give back to the community.

Aziza RAJAB
CES Kenya Director

My Dad, Rajab Mwenje, happened to be among the founding members. He served for ten years as the Vice Chairman of CES in Kenya. When he passed on in 2014, we thought our family should go on supporting the schools. So I began sponsoring some students, and soon after that Michael and Malik thought it would be prudent to have me as a member of the Board. Given my age and life experience, I could offer mentorship and a youth perspective.

So, how are we doing regarding the plan and objectives of CES Kenya? In my view we've done great. It's been only three years for me being on the Board, and I have actually seen some transformation. Some students who are in the junior years of high school are being supported until the end of school, and coming out of school with very good grades. I have seen schools where CES has created special projects such as teaching the importance of hand-washing, and supporting agriculture including dairy farms. The students are very grateful, because most of them come from very poor backgrounds, and without a scholarship, they'd be rotting in their village.

But here we're helping create doctors, engineers, teachers and farmers and the impact is actually very big. Consider one of our female university students; without the help of CES, she would be in the village, married with maybe three children. The reality in western Kenya for women is that if you finish Form Four, you don't have any future going forward. The next thing is, you're going to get married to a person who is poorer than you, so you're just producing babies. You don't have any options or other economic opportunities. By the time you're thirty, you have five children and no income. Or maybe you work as house help or something like that.

Mzungu asks, "can you describe the gradual transition of CES from supporting mostly high school students to one that supports students through university?"

It does reduce opportunities for high school students, but university education is also not very accessible. Right now, the government is trying to subsidize high school education. They say it is 'free,' but it is not. So we need to have a new strategy. High school is a more affordable right now, and much better than it was some years ago.

University, on the other hand, is not. And then again, the national government's support is in the form of a loan, which you have to repay. So with CES taking a new direction, now sponsoring university education, it's a move in the right direction. Let's see how it goes. The program is a bit flexible and has strong potential.

CES Kenya is establishing a pilot project between now and 2022, and we will be assessing as it goes along. So as we finish that particular phase, we can see the impact. We can determine if there is still a need for high school students to be sponsored; we can always go back, there is that flexibility. That's because at the end of the day, we do this for and in the interests of our students.

CHAPTER 20:
Responding to a Changing World

"Charity is a matter of the heart, not of the pocket"

Kenyan proverb

Kenya is undergoing a number of education reforms in both curriculum design and the new 2-6-3-3-3 school operational system. Since 1984, the 8-4-4 (Primary/Secondary/Tertiary) model has been the norm. Over the past three years there has been much debate about a new format that gives added focus to elementary education and less to secondary and tertiary studies. Despite the challenges and inconsistencies associated with implementation, Kenya continues to produce outstanding students who shine and excel in academics. Among these are CES Canada/Kenya graduates who now are in higher learning institutions studying in China and in universities and colleges throughout Kenya.

By contrast, there are children and youth that never have had a chance to attend and achieve learning benchmarks. There are a number of factors that prevent students from completing even the basic primary level of education. Only 40% of students achieving the KCPE will go on to and complete the standardized KCSE exams that lead to a high school diploma. This 'socio-economic tragedy' is compounded as 1.2 million orphans in

Kenya struggle each day to survive. Education is never a priority when the basic needs of life are not met.

Three key factors hinder the equality of educational opportunities for Kenyan youth:

POVERTY

Despite free education in primary schools and a government subsidy for secondary education, acute poverty keeps children home. University education is expensive and is reserved for the few who can afford it. Orphaned youth and others whose parents cannot afford to pay school fees become marginalized. Students from poverty-stricken areas are faced with environmental calamities and diseases such as malaria, tuberculosis and HIV/AIDS. Those who attend school have few reading and learning resources and classes often take place in overcrowded classrooms.

GENDER INEQUALITY

The issue of gender creates an imbalance of opportunity. A boy will be educated when there are only funds for one in the family to attend school. Societal roles dictate that education is of little value for the girl child. In areas of upper Rift Valley, North-East and Coast Counties, some girls are married off at a very young age. Boys in nomadic tribal areas are expected to herd animals. The Kenyan government places a heavy penalty for any parent that bars a child from education. However, the reality is that too many children are denied their education.

PEER PRESSURE and DRUG ABUSE

Substance abuse of cocaine, heroin, bhang, khat and alcohol is common among youth. This creates a society where more students drop out of school, and unemployment increases. Communities then deal with the statistics that emerge from HIV/AIDS, teenage pregnancy and prostitution. There is little hope that remains after these have taken their toll.

Kenya recorded close to 40% unemployment according to a recent report by the United Nations: *Human Development Index (HDI) 2017*. The actual figure for youth under age 25 is an alarming 60%, due to a difficult economic environment. Kenya has the highest unemployment rate in East Africa, with countries like Ethiopia, Tanzania, Uganda and Rwanda doing better. Kenya is a country in crisis and it does not appear that the situation will turn around in time for the next generation to see the benefits of stronger economic growth.

CES Canada believes in the importance of education, inclusivity, equal opportunity and gender equality. All youth are considered to be equal and must be free from the prejudice associated with disability, ethnic or religious background, sexual orientation, or economic status. To that end, CES has created scholarships, mentoring and training programs, ICT Learning programs and Leadership Development Programs for young people orphaned by the HIV/AIDS pandemic living in rural western Kenya.

During its first ten years of operation, CES Canada focused on scholarships for secondary students. It was cost efficient and there were many more students than could be assisted. The message was consistent that CES would only support students up to and including Form Four (final year of high school) and completion of the KCSE (Kenya Certificate of Secondary Education). After that, it was up to students to make it on their own.

Having been orphaned and knowing a life of financial struggle, few were attending and completing higher learning. It seemed such a waste of talent and opportunity. Many CES graduates applied at universities across Kenya. They were accepted for registration but that's as far as it went for them. They did not have the financial resources to attend.

There has been, in the past five years, a growing feeling that Kenyan students, although talented and bright, were ill prepared for the real world of work. Although they had succeeded in an education environment that stressed memorization of facts, students were not able to communicate, problem solve, work as a group, or show initiative. As well, they lacked self-confidence. That is what started the whole curriculum review and the perceived need to change the system entirely.

At the same time, CES Canada was evaluating its effectiveness as a charity. We realized that our best and brightest were at a standstill and denied the university education they were capable of completing.

There was a strong intent to do as much as we could do through partial scholarships. Students could apply and be interviewed according to their need and ability to pursue higher learning.

From 2013-19, CES has provided 153 partial scholarships and thirty full scholarships at the undergraduate and post graduate levels. Students have also had opportunity to participate in Leadership Training through the CES School of Continuing Education (CESCED).

The intent was to provide CES Graduates with a chance to become fully employable in the major professions; in Business, Science and Technology, Agriculture, Water Management, Medicine, Community Health, Social Services and Education. Being part of an on-line leadership training program has also provided IT and personal development skills that allow our graduates to compete with top students across the country and around the world. Our vision to equip and enable youth to become leaders and nation builders has now become the main reason why there is less emphasis on providing resources for secondary education.

To make a contribution towards the development and strengthening of rural communities in Kenya is critical to what CES considers its ongoing mandate. Although it is possible to do both, on balance and recognizing the challenges of funding programs, CES is now pursuing scholarship programs at the Post-Secondary level. There will be funding for clean water, nutrition and health related initiatives; however, there are no capital investment strategies considered for infrastructure within the twenty-five school communities CES is currently involved in.

2019 is a momentous year for CES Canada. As we enter our 15th year of service to rural western Kenya, it is important to reflect on our history and to thank those who have supported this initiative. In the years to come, it will be said that our legacy was to provide thousands of Kenyan youth with hope for a brighter future. CES Canada is also part of a larger picture where Canadian NGO's and faith-based organizations are making huge global humanitarian contributions.

Since 2004, Community Education Services (CES) Canada has been providing hope through education for youth orphaned by HIV/AIDS living in Kenya. Things are changing and we are making a difference.

CES Canada can be defined in part by its spirit of openness, inclusiveness, cooperation, and friendship. The world needs a heart that beats for the downtrodden. It needs people who are passionate about change and transforming unacceptable realities; it needs Canada, and it needs CES Canada.

There are no small players on the stage of humanitarian aid and international development. All contributions add to the total picture of building and equipping communities and nations around the world. It is important for CES to grow as a charity and also to be sensitive to the tides of social change. Youth unemployment in Kenya is more critical than ever. Youth as a whole are discouraged and have lost their way. They look to their leaders for the way forward, not realizing that the way forward can be found within themselves.

Transformation in society is a long process involving two to three generations led by strong vision and positive actions. Creating a small group of agents for change has now become the way for CES Canada to make a difference. Time will reveal its legacy; hopefully, it will hopefully be said one day, that a small group of CES graduates became a powerful force for good in Kenya.

Fate Finally Fades to Hope

Our fate was to walk in the wilderness,
to rummage among rubbish bins,
with worry and despair evident on our faces,
they now begin to fade in the light of education.
Left behind by more fortunate colleagues,
we floundered in a world where school uniforms
and other requirements for learning were unknown to us.
The roots of Canadian scholarships fanned out,
spreading its shade towards the poor and needy.
we now enjoy the fruits of this generosity.
The beautiful buildings of our schools,
clean water projects, battery toothbrushes,
solar rechargeable lamps, mosquito nets, backpacks,
sanitary towels and of course school fees paid,
have nullified the grand challenges to education,
so now we are learning.
As our fate fades, traces of its scent still remain.
We are faced with challenges for emerging issues,
illness and rampant absenteeism die to fees' constraints
that sting us like scorpions.

Hail the CES organization that breathes life to us,
hail our dear school administration,
for they encourage us to be at our best.
We are young seedlings nourished
by the well drained soils of learning,
like bees we sing the sweetest song,
like the tailor, forming a great stitch in time
that hence could save nine.
Our fate has finally faded - a new hope in its place.

Sheila Nasindu, Teacher
CES Grad 2012 - Musaga SS
09/2012

ADDENDUM:

Community Education Services (CES) Canada (est. 2004)
"providing access to secondary education for
Kenyan youth orphaned by HIV/AIDS"

In Partnership with:

- Community Education Services (CES) Kenya (est. 2005)
- Masinde Muliro University of Science and Technology (MMUST) (est.2014)

In Association with:

- ACCES Africa Canada Continuing Education Society (2008)
- Divine Providence Orphanage, Kakamega (2010)
- EAAPP East Africa Agriculture Production Project (2013)
- KEEF Kenya Education Endowment Fund (2015)
- The Peter Cundill Foundation (2013)
- UNICEF Wash In Schools WinS Program (2012)
- UN Economic & Social Council (ECOSOC) (2013)
- Water Mission International (2015)
- World Without Worms Canada (2012)

EDUCATION Provided:

- Secondary Scholarships in 45 Schools
- 3000 secondary school scholarships/750 graduates
- 120 Post Secondary Scholarships - Middle Colleges/Universities
- 15 CES Leadership Scholarships
- CESCED (CES School of Continuing Education)
- Healthy Living/Career Development Seminars
- ICT Learning Program (2015-18)
- Scholarship Leadership Development Program
- Internship Teacher Education Training Program
- CES Alumni Group (CBO)
- CES Form 4 Senior Advisory Group

- Community Health Services Outreach
- CES Alumni Community Outreach
- CES Consultants — Education, Sports, Persons of Disability
- CES Advisory Team - Education, Community Health, Environment, Agriculture

WATER Served:

- UNICEF Global Outreach (WASH in SCHOOLS - WinS)
- Research (Hygiene/Water Management)
- Hand Washing Station (Kimang'eti Girls SS 2015-16)
- Water Station (Namirama Girls HS 2017)
- Clean Water projects at 9 rural schools
- CES Grad – Advisor, Water and Environment Sustainability

HEALTH PROGRAMS Delivered:

- PAD Feminine Hygiene for all CES Female Students
- De-Worming Community Outreach (2013) for 50,000 Children
- IC2 Read Vision Project (2015) - Ingotse Medical Clinic 300 Patients
- Anti-Malaria Mosquito Nets for all CES Students
- Personal Hygiene/Health Kits (2013-18)
- 3 Jiggers Campaigns (2016-17) – 1000 children treated
- CES Grad – Advisor, Community Health

NUTRITION Promoted:

- Dairy farm / Agriculture projects at four secondary schools
- Poultry farm at St Mary Goretti Girls HS at Shikoti
- CES Grad – Advisor, Agriculture and Farm Management

INFRASTRUCTURE Built:

- Musaga SS with enrolment of 480 students
- St. Agnes Dormitory at St. Mary Goretti Girls HS Shikoti
- 2 Science Labs - Ibinzo SS and Navakholo SS
- 2 Computer Labs - Namirama Girls HS and Navakholo SS
- Kitchen / Dining Room - Eshitari SS, Musaga SS

RESEARCH:

- Impact of HIV/AIDS on Kenya School System (2004)
- Feminine Hygiene Study in CES-associated schools (2009)
- Design: N.Nuk/S.Michalowicz
- Participatory Development Planning and Economic Self Determination (2011) at Ileho, Kenya in collaboration with Cynthia Abatt, U of Massachusetts
- Knowledge, Attitude and Practice of Secondary School Students on Water Hygiene Sanitation (2013) in collaboration with Masinde Muliro University of Science and Technology (MMUST)
- Report to Int'l Conference - UN SDG's 2030 at MMUST: Paper by CES Kenya Grad Busuku Musli on "Communicable Diseases" (2015)
- Report to Int'l Conference – UN SDG's 2030 at MMUST: Paper by CES Kenya Grad Philice Musundi on "Peace and Reconciliation" (2015)

SPECIAL PROJECTS:

CES Christmas Projects:

- Edu-Packs for Learning Project (2006)
- Anti-Malaria Mosquito Net Project (2007)
- Solar Lamps Project (2008)
- CES Kenya PAD Project Project (2009)
- Reforestation Environment Project (2010)
- CES Kenya Ambassadors Program (2011)
- Bishop Sulumeti Girls HS Library Project (2012)
- Divine Providence Orphanage School Uniform Project (2014)
- Hygiene Health Kit (2015-19)

Coordinated Initiatives:

- Canada Day Run (2011-2019)
- CES Wash in Schools Project (2014-19)
- CES PAD (Feminine Hygiene) Education Program (2009-19)
- CES Kenya Reforestation Project (2010)
- Bishop Sulumeti Girls HS Library Project (2012)

- Raising Resilience Arts Project (2013)
- Musaga SS Hydro Project (2013)
- CES Kenya 140 Km Peace Run/Rally for Peace (2013)
- Navakholo County De-Worming Project - 50,000 children (2013)
- IC2 Read Eyewear Project (2014-15)
- CES Jiggers Medical Outreach Project (2016-17)

Major Building Projects:

- Musaga Secondary School (2010-16)
- Eshitari SS Kitchen Project (2012-14)
- St Mary Goretti Girls HS St Agnes Dorm Project (2012-13)
- Musaga SS Kitchen Project (2015-16)

Special Interest Initiatives:

- Divine Providence Orphanage, Kakamega (2011-19)
- Teacher Exchange - Bishop Sulumeti Girls HS, Kakamega and Longfields-Davidson Heights SS Nepean, Ontario (2012)

Key Events/Conferences:

2008 HIV/AIDS Awareness/Healthy Living
2009 Education Planning
2010 Volunteers/Service
2011 Career Choices
2012 Substance Abuse
2013 CES Kenya Peace Run/Rally (Kericho-Kakamega)
2013 Celebration of Faith (St Agnes Thunder Bay/Bishop Sulumeti Kakamega Parish)
2014 10th Anniversary Celebrations
2015 Leadership Training
2016 Career and Educational Planning
2017 Leadership Development
2018 Celebrating Leaders in Education (CES Principals/ Head Teachers)
2018 Form 4 Conference Leadership Development
2019 Preparing for Higher Learning

Writer's Workshops:

2011-2012 & 2015 CES Kenya Poetry/Prose Writing Competition

Well Projects:

2010 Eshitari SS
2011 Ematiha SS
2011 Musaga PS
2012 Navakholo SS
2012 Khachonge PS
2012 Kumugui SS
2013 Namundera SS
2014 Divine Providence Orphanage
2019 St Caroli Lwanga Lutaso SS

Agri-Farm Projects:

2010 Navakholo SS
2013 Bishop Sulumeti Girls HS
2014 St Mary Goretti Girls HS Shikoti
2016 Namirama Girls HS

Reforestation Projects:

2010 Namirama Girls HS
2010 Bishop Sulumeti Girls HS
2019 Masinde Muliro University of Science and Technology

ICT Education Skills Training Project:

2014 St Patrick's Ikonyero SS
2015 Bishop Sulumeti GHS, Shieywe SS, Kakamega Muslim SS
2015 Namirama Girls SS, Navakholo SS, St Caroli Lwanga Lutaso SS
2016 Buhayi Muslim SS, Friends Sidikho SS, Namundera SS
2017 Bukhakunga SS, Musaga SS, Sivilie SS
2017 St Mary Goretti Shikoti Girls HS, Bushiri SS, Lirhanda Girls HS
2018 St Peter's Mwiruti SS, Lions HS, St Cecilia Misikhu Girls HS,
Kimang'eti Girls HS,

2018 St Jude Napara Girls SS, Makhukuni SS, Inaya SS, St Jan Kimilili SS

CES Internship Program:

2011 to 2019 - 76 students

CES Leadership On-Line Training Program:

CES School of Continuing Education (CESCED)
2015 to 2019 - G7 - Mashujaa (Heroes for Change)
2018 to 2022 - G7 - Viongozi (Leaders in Action)

CES Schools * Residential Boarding

Bishop Sulumeti Girls HS*
Buhayi Muslim SS
Bushiri SS
Ematiha SS
Eshitari SS (2008-14)
Ibinzo Girls SS (2007-14)
Inaya SS
Kakamega Muslim SS
Kilimo Girls HS (2010-14)
Kimang'eti Girls HS*
Lions HS (Kisumu)
Lirhanda Girls HS*
Makhukuni SS
Musaga SS
Namirama Girls HS*
Namundera SS
Navakholo SS
Samitsi SS
Shieywe SS
Sidikho SS
St Mary Goretti Girls HS*
Sivilie SS
St. Caroli Lwanga Lutaso SS

St. Jan Kimilili SS

St. Patrick's Bukhakunha SS

St. Patrick's Ikonyero SS

St. Peter Mwiruti Girls HS*

St. Jude SS Napara

St. Cecilia Girls HS Misikhu*

CES Expansion Project (2011-15)

Thika School for the Blind (Thika)

Bwake SS (Bungoma)

St. Jan SS (Bungoma)

Loreto Nakuru SS (Nakuru)

Kumugui SS (Bungoma)

Maryhill Girls HS (Thika)

St. Mary's Yala SS (Yala)

Nkubu SS (Meru)

Sheikh Ali SS (Mandera)

Ngara Girls (Nairobi)

Moi Girls Nangili (Eldoret)

Kadika Girls SS (Migori)

Makueni Boys SS (Wote)

Nyamiranga SS (Mokomoni)

Tombee SS (Kisii)

THANKS AND APPRECIATION

The Peter Cundill Foundation (est. 2012) honours the legacy of renowned Canadian philanthropist, F. Peter Cundill, (1938-2011). The Foundation has an emphasis on promoting the health, education and well-being of young people. CES Canada gratefully acknowledges the funding (2013 to present) received for its key initiatives: secondary and post secondary scholarships, the Lutaso Well Project, the ICT Mobile Lab Learning Project and the CES School of Continuing Education Leadership Program.

CES Canada acknowledges the support of the Canada Running Series. Since 2008, CES Canada has participated in the Scotiabank Toronto Waterfront Marathon Charity Challenge (STWM). As a result, Team CESCAN has provided 1200 secondary scholarships and 3500 athletic shoes to needy youth in Kenya.

CES Canada gratefully acknowledges the many donors and volunteers without whom CES could not exist.

Partners and friends that constitute the CES family and who continue to support our mission to Kenya include:

- Allan Skidmore Family Foundation
- Jessoma Foundation
- Moody's Foundation
- Poul Due Jensen Foundation, Denmark
- The Peter Cundill Foundation
- Canada Helps
- Canada Running Series CRS
- CES Canada and CES Kenya Board of Directors
- CESCED School of Continuing Education
- CES Scholars and CES Leadership Group
- CES Canada Chapter Executive Thunder Bay ON, Hampton NB, Ottawa ON, Kyoto Japan
- CES Kenya Alumni Executive
- Church of the Redeemer, Rosseau ON
- Etobicoke Dental Health Centre
- Extreme Imaging, Barrie ON
- Georgian Copy and Printers, Barrie ON
- Kingsway Baptist Church, Toronto ON
- KKP Etobicoke
- Masinde Muliro University of Science and Technology (MMUST)
- Mojazima Inc. Sport Africa
- New Balance Canada
- Sheywe Conference Centre Kakamega KENYA
- Volunteers to Kenya
- Water Mission

CONTRIBUTORS

Michael Frederiksen
Founder CES Canada

Michael Frederiksen immigrated to Canada from Denmark in 1951. His career in education spans thirty-five years as teacher and administrator at the elementary, secondary and post secondary levels of education. He has worked on a number of international humanitarian and educational projects in Kenya, India, Pakistan and Grenada. In 2004 Michael was instrumental in founding CES and presently is a member of its board of directors. He is a strong advocate for children with disabilities, particularly those who suffer from polio and HIV/AIDS.

Malik Khaemba, Hsc
Patron, CES Kenya

Malik Khaemba has served as the Patron of CES Kenya since 2004. Previously Malik served for two decades (1985-20015) as a diplomat with Kenya Foreign Affairs in Abu Dhabi, Brussels and Ottawa Canada. In 2008 Malik Khaemba was appointed to Kakamega County to sensitize rural communities and help bring in the new Kenyan Constitution. He has been honoured with the distinction of 'HSC' Head of State Commendation, awarded by the President of Kenya. Malik is the CEO and a founding member of CES Kenya.

Patricia Makori
Principal CES School of Continuing Education and Director, CES Kenya

Patricia studied at University of Nairobi and graduated with an MBA and a post graduate Diploma in Human Resource Management. Patricia's support of gender based projects has been recognized through the CES Canada Award of Excellence in Education (2016). A keen advocate for human rights and global education, she has worked in community health and education projects for nearly two decades. The impact of her humanitarian work in Kenya has been felt through the Nomadic Girls Rescue Centre in

Turkana County, the Kenya Red Cross, Community Education Services (CES) Kenya and Good Vision Glasses. She is a member of the Kenya Psychological Counselling Association.

Sarah Nabongo
CES Kenya Executive Office Manager

Sarah Nabongo brings many years of experience working in the area of community services. Since 2012 she has served as CES Kenya office administrator and front line contact for visitors. Her expertise in IT computer communications has provided valuable assistance to CES Canada. Sarah manages special events and finds time to work on projects such as the CES Health Hygiene Kits and PAD project. She works closely with CES students to ensure their accountability and success. She holds a Diploma in Business Administration and a Bachelor of Commerce Degree - Human Resources from Jomo Kenyatta University of Agriculture and Technology.

Tom Conant
CES Canada Director and Project Coordinator

Tom Conant graduated in 2010 from McGill University in International Studies. After extensive travels in South East Asia he taught ESL in South Korea. During 2012 and 2013 Tom travelled to Kenya on two occasions and there established himself as a key member of the CES Kenya team. His experience in the field includes teaching assignments in CES schools and the establishment of the Oasis of Learning Library at the Bishop Sulumeti Girls HS in Kakamega. Tom coordinated four major projects in Kenya; CES De-Worming Project with outreach of 50,000 primary school children, 2013 CES Kenya Peace Run, the Hydro project at Musaga SS and the Library Project at Bishop Sulumeti Girls HS. Tom continues his work with CES as a Director, advising and helping to establish projects on the ground.

Carl Friesen

CES Canada Board member

Carl has a background in journalism and editing, including work with community newspapers, daily newspapers, magazines and online media. He holds a BA in Geography, an Honours BA in Journalism, and an MBA from the University of Toronto. He is the author of five published books on the subject of content marketing for professional firms. As part of his work as a communications consultant, Carl has written articles for international publications and helped his clients publish several books of their own. He is a frequent public speaker on marketing and business strategy. Carl travelled to Kenya in September 2018 primarily to interview Kenyans in preparation of this book.

GLOSSARY

Asante – Thank you

Boda Boda – Bicycle taxi commonly in Kenya to carry people and goods

Form One to Form Four – Equivalent to high school or secondary school in North America – Grades 9 through 12

Harambee – A Swahili expression for 'pull together', an unofficial motto for much of East Africa

Kidogo kidogo – A Swahili expression for 'little by little', often referring to the pace of change in Kenya

KCPE – Kenya Certificate of Primary Education, a national examination which all graduating students must pass in order to receive their diploma from elementary school

KCSE – Kenya Certificate of Secondary Education, a national examination for secondary school students

Karibu – welcome (also, you're welcome)

Kenyan Shilling – Common currency (100 Shillings is equal to $1US and $.75Cdn)

Kiswahili – a trade language widely spoken throughout East Africa – including Uganda, Kenya, Tanzania and the eastern DR Congo. Sometimes it gets shortened to "Swahili"

Matatu – a mini bus (seats up to 14 persons) common in Kenya as a mode of transportation

Mwalimu – teacher

Mzungu – An East African term for a white person or people of European descent.

Pikipiki – motorcycle taxi used to transport goods and people

Standard One to Eight – Equivalent to elementary school in North America – Grades 1 through 8

Ugali – a staple food in East Africa, ground corn made into a thick porridge, usually served with vegetables, seasoning and sometimes meat or fish

CPSIA information can be obtained
at www.ICGtesting.com
Printed in the USA
BVHW092140191220
596040BV00004B/34

9 781525 559419